Robert Munro

Minor Poems and Translations in Verse,

from admired compositions of the ancient Celtic bards, with the Gaelic, and

illustrative notes

Robert Munro

Minor Poems and Translations in Verse,
from admired compositions of the ancient Celtic bards, with the Gaelic, and illustrative notes

ISBN/EAN: 9783337295752

Printed in Europe, USA, Canada, Australia, Japan

Cover: Foto ©Thomas Meinert / pixelio.de

More available books at **www.hansebooks.com**

MINOR POEMS,

AND

TRANSLATIONS, IN VERSE,

FROM ADMIRED COMPOSITIONS OF

THE ANCIENT CELTIC BARDS;

With the Gaelic,

AND ILLUSTRATIVE NOTES.

BY ROBERT MUNRO.

SECOND ISSUE.

"It must strike every impartial inquirer into the subject, that the Collectors of the ancient, or supposed ancient, compositions of the Highlands have produced to the world poetry which, in sublimity and tenderness, will, it is believed, be admitted to be at least equal to the compositions of the best modern poets, and but little inferior to the most admired among the ancient."—HENRY MACKENZIE, *in Report of Highland Society's Committee on Ossian.*

EDINBURGH:
PRINTED FOR THE AUTHOR.

MDCCCLXIX.

TO HIS GRACE

THE DUKE OF RICHMOND AND LENNOX, K. G.

PRESIDENT OF THE HIGHLAND SOCIETY OF SCOTLAND,

THIS VOLUME IS,

WITH HIS GRACE'S PERMISSION,

HUMBLY INSCRIBED.

CONTENTS.

	PAGE
TO THE SEA,	1
THE DESERTED VALLEY,	7
THE ESCAPE OF MARY QUEEN OF SCOTS FROM LOCHLEVEN CASTLE,	12
TO THE RUINS OF CROOKSTON CASTLE,	16
THE STORY OF LIFE,	20
"SHE TOLD NOT HER SORROW,"	23
THE IMPROVIDENT,	25
TO A HOUSE FLY,	27
A DREAM OF LOST JOY,	30
THE MOURNER'S SONG,	34
STANZAS—"HOW SHOULD I MURMUR AT THE HOUR,"	36
LINES—"AWAKE ONCE MORE, THOU SIMPLE LYRE,"	38
THE TEAR-DROP OF JOY,	40
FIRST LOVE,	41
TO THE FALSE,	43
LUGANO,	45

CONTENTS.

	PAGE
THE BROKEN SWORD, A TRADITIONARY TALE OF CULLODEN,	48
SONG—"THE HIGHLAND GARB,"	59
SONG—"BY CLYDE'S CLEAR STREAM,"	62
THE WANDERER,	64
EPISTLE TO A FRIEND,	67
LINES WRITTEN IN A CHURCH-YARD IN A LONELY SCENE OF THE HIGHLANDS,	72
"THE HOURS I THINK OF THEE,"	73
THE NORE,	74
LINES, ON A VIEW OF THE COVENANTERS' TOMB IN THE BOG OF LOCH IN-KETT, GALLOWAY,	75
POLITICAL ERROR,	76

TRANSLATIONS FROM THE CELTIC.

	PAGE
THE AGED BARD'S WISH,	79
MIANN A BHAIRD AOSDA,	81
NOTES,	100
THE DEATH OF CARRIL,	103
BAS CHAIREILL,	105
NOTES,	114
FAINASOLLIS,	116
FAINE SOLUIS,	119
NOTES,	128
FRITHIL,	131
FRAOCH,	133
EXTRACT FROM DERMID,	148
AS-TARRUINN O' DHIARMAD,	149
EXTRACTS FROM GAUL,	152
EXTRACT FROM THE DEATH OF OSSIAN,	163
OSSIAN'S ADDRESS TO THE SUN, FROM THE ORIGINAL,	168
DUAN OISEIN DO'N GHREIN,	169
ULLIN'S ADDRESS TO THE SUN,	174
DUAN EILE DO'N GHREIN—LE ULAIN,	175
MALVINA'S DREAM,	176
AISLIN MHALMHINE,	179

POEMS AND TRANSLATIONS.

TO THE SEA.

O BEAUTIFUL, O faithless Sea!
   Thou peerless in magnificence—
Thou darkest in fatality!
   Heaven be his stay and sure defence
Who trusteth in thy constancy!

The hardy one, who, for a life
   Of little joy and frequent strife,
Upon thy changeful breast to roam,
   Hath bartered all the sweets of home,—
When years have dimmed his lustrous eye
   And silvered o'er his raven hair,
And spared his life to linger by
   The hearth his childhood loved to share,

In words of truth will oft declare
    How much his checkered days have known
Of pleasure unalloyed by care,
    And wretchedness and care anon ;
And of thy ever-changing mood,
    In many a winning hour will tell,
How furious now, and now subdued
    By love and pity, prove thee well—
So deadly in thine influence—
So fair in thy magnificence—
So twined, through safety and through scaith,
With life, and loveliness, and death !

The mariner, how blest with peace,
When winds and waves their tumults cease !
What time, becalmed, his bark must rest
Upon thy calm and tranquil breast,
In solitude, in summer time,
In some serene and orient clime,
Where western zephyrs oft repair
To rest their weary pinions there !

That mariner, how light at heart
To watch successive suns depart,
As oft restoring to his view
The blest monotony of blue !

Then absence of his wonted cares
To fond affection stronger bears
The forms in faithful memory set—
The soil he never will forget!

He paces much the well-trimmed bark,
And views the long familiar mark;
Or, lounging on the prostrate sail,
Lists to a messmate's curious tale;
Or wistfully he travels o'er
The pages of romantic lore;
Or strives in useful sport to slay
The feathered or the finny prey;
Or from the flute he wins a strain
That cheers the heart with pleasing pain.

And when long days of musing past
Have brought him tedious hours at last,
To steer away he would be fain,
And whistles for the breeze in vain.
Then, thoughtful bending o'er to view
In thee his rude form mirrored true,
Thee for no adverse fate he blames,
But yields the love a parent claims.

O ever changing, faithless Sea !
When thou putt'st off tranquillity—
When peace and beauty are estranged,
And thy mild aspect darkly changed.
To revel in a deadly hour
Thou dost awake thy wrathful power,—
O then, oppressed by every care,
How wretched is the mariner !

When darkening clouds are low'ring nigh,
And rising winds impetuous fly,
The seaman dreads thy coming wrath ;
Then, fearful of his dangerous path,
Would only seek a friendly shore
To rest him till thy fit passed o'er ;
Then track thy bosom o'er again.
Give thee his love, and thine regain.

Though guiltless of a crime 'gainst thee,
Though trusting thy fidelity—
In hour of dread to thee confined
A friendly shore he may not find ;
For thou, to have his purpose stay'd,
Wilt ruthless summon to thine aid
The bursting winds that wander nigh,
Obedient to thy revelry !

TO THE SEA.

When torturing hours do still unfold
Thy liquid waste of alpine mould ;
When anguish rends his stricken breast,
And grief and toil alike molest ;
And yet no cheering prospect nigh,
No kindred mourner wandering by,
And hope and pity almost gone,
And he must toil and weep alone ;—
Then how thy wild laugh mocks his cry,—
His vain demand for sympathy !

In that dread hour, when to his sight,
Like warriors plumed for vengeful fight,
Thy mountain-waves come wildly on,
 Deadly destructive, one by one,
Then fame and fortune he'd forego,
Nay, murmur not at many a woe ;
But O he'd have thee stay thy strife,
And spare his little span of life !

And when at length divides away
His beaten bark—his cherished stay—
And he has felt that little space
Must bear him to thy cold embrace,

He meets thy mighty murdering billow
With only this to smooth his pillow—
That all his griefs are past !

If there is aught in Nature's plan
That might awake regret in man,
It is, O witching, wanton deep !
To gaze on thy mysterious sleep,
When thou, beneath a summer sky,
Subdued to very love, dost lie,
And know, that influence to impair
Man's little joy, existed there !

THE DESERTED VALLEY.

Once, long ago, with dreamy joy,
   I hail'd the summer-scented gale
That wafted me—light-hearted boy—
   Afar from thee—my native vale.

Our light bark bounded o'er the wave,
   The sea-bird shriek'd its evening spell;
And I, unheard, but fondly, gave
   To thee and thine a long farewell!

I soon forgot (to think of't now!)
   Thy woodland paths and murm'ring rills;
I in a distant land, and thou
   Reposing 'midst green Albion's hills.

I soon forgot, while many a change
   Broke on my view, for I was free
To breast the proud Alps' mighty range,
   Or bask in sunny Italy.

Successive seasons lightly passed;
  My steps by youthful fancy led,
And visionary joys; at last,
  I thought of thee, sweet Stanlymead!

I thought of thee,—no idle joy
  Can long subdue our thoughts of home.
Nor pleasure's airy wand destroy
  Those haunts where memory loves to roam.

A wanderer in those lovely climes
  Where eastern zephyrs gently glide,
I've listened to the vesper chimes,
  Thought of my Scottish home, and sighed!

In scenes where luxury instals
  The dazzling state of orient pride,
Remembrance of my fathers' halls
  Has turned the vain display aside.

My simple heart was oft beguiled
  By witchery of woman's eye;
And artful beauty, too, has smiled,
  To prompt that heart's inconstancy.

But while the influence strove to dwell,
   And parting reason still delayed,
One imaged charm dissolved the spell,—
   My country's modest mountain maid !

Oft on the deep, in eves of June,
   I've leant beneath the slumb'ring sail ;
The blue waves murmuring to the moon—
   I musing on my native vale.

Years passed away—full forty times—
   My country smiled in summer's glow ;
And still I sought in other climes
   What it could much and well bestow.

But prudence came with youth's decay,
   And taught my long deluded eye
That pleasure was a transient ray,
   And false its winning witchery.

Then truant fancy would be fain
   Once more amidst thy wilds to stray :
Hope whispered fond salutes again,
   And sweetly cheered my homeward way.

O yes! the charmer lent her guile,
    And promised me of joy, no less
Than meet again affection's smile,
    And friendship's gentle hand to press.

In vain, alas! A mournful change
    Decayed thy beauties; time's career
Had faded thy fair fertile range,
    And banish'd all I held so dear!

The woodland boughs were spreading still,
    The crag-topp'd banks were green as ever;
The torrent leaped adown the hill,
    A silv'ry tribute to the river:

But lonely now appeared the wood,
    As hollow breezes swept its deepness;
Fled from the banks the bleating brood
    That skipped before across their steepness.

And on the hill, beside the font—
    Nor through the brook—nor by the river,
Mused,—sported,—or waysped as wont,
    The learned, the artless, or the lover.

I sought the little dear retreat,
　Where many a simple tale was heard :
'Twas sad to see the proud thorns meet,
　And trample on its velvet sward !

I paced our old ancestral halls :
　The yielding timbers creaked beneath ;
The cold wind whistled through their walls—
　O but it seemed the home of death !

An evil destiny's dark hand
　Had left its trace in our fair grove ;
And death had brought his dreadful brand,
　And hushed the voice of kindred love !

THE ESCAPE OF MARY QUEEN OF SCOTS FROM LOCHLEVEN CASTLE.

The faithful and brave of her kingdom have sought her,
    Their prayers are useless,—their threats are in vain :
The Murray is proud, and the Douglas has bought her,
    And lowly she pines in a merciless chain :—
O see ye yon water by mountains surrounded ?
    And see ye yon tower on its bosom so fair ?
That water is deep,—and these walls iron-bounded,—
    The Flower of fair Scotland in thraldom is there !

From Edina's bright halls the hard hearted have borne her—
    From gladness and grandeur, and courtly array,
And lords and fair maidens all silently mourn her—
    Their Queen, their devoted, their beautiful May !
That smile is now lost in the heavings of sorrow—
    That love-beaming eye is oppressed by a tear—
A captive she pines,—but there's hope on the morrow,—
    And *one* who would die for her freedom is near.

The willow-tree weeps on the marge of Lochleven,
 The field is deserted—forsaken the bower ;
And the fair moon looks down from her palace in Heaven,
 To bless with her radiance the languishing flower.—
Who lonely is he on the castle's high summit
 So stately, surveying the charms that are nigh ?
Ha ! gallant George Douglas ! fate grant thou mays't win it,—
 There's love in thy bosom—there's hope in thine eye !

He hasteneth thence while a taper is brightening
 The iron-barred lattice where Mary has wept,
And the signal that gleams in the woodland like lightning
 Tells of fealty untired, and of constancy kept !
On mountain and moorland a stillness is reigning,
 No murmur is heard, and no wanderer seen—
The portals are fast, and the warder is dreaming,—
 O little he wots of the moment, I ween !

" The dove will not perch on the eagle's wild eyrie—
 The rose will not blossom where reptiles are free !
These halls of my kindred are friendless and dreary,
 And not, my loved Sovereign, a dwelling for thee.—
But I, of my tribe, would rejoice to restore thee
 To bowers where oppression will cease to annoy—
Even now the glad hour of departure is o'er thee,—
 O haste, my liege lady, to freedom and joy !"

* * * * * *

A dear laden boat from the island is stealing—
   Lo! swiftly it sweeps o'er the waters so blue—
In vain are the castle's dark battlements pealing—
   Those arms will row well as that bosom beats true!
The moonlight shines forth, and the breezes come stronger :—
   O merrily row, nor delay—nor despair—
There is wildness in yonder grey tower, for no longer
   The Flower of fair Scotland in thraldom is there!

On yon strand are bold knights with their proud steeds
   awaiting,
   Bright corselets protect gallant bosoms and true;
All doubts now depart, and new hopes are creating—
   The billow that bears the high prize bursts to view!
Joy! joy! she is free! the good father is breathing
   To Heaven the thanks of each glad cavalier!
The steeds are impatient—the swords are unsheathing—
   Why linger with danger, the moment is dear?

" O Douglas! seek not this frail hand with thy wooing—
   Its joys and its sorrows another must share—
Though well be thy meed—and though earnest thy suing—
   Yet, turn to yon ambush—thy Marion is there!—

Yes! she doth await thee to whom thou art plighted—
   Her love be thy guerdon—to her thou art dear,
Nor rashly aspire, lest her fondness be blighted!"
   Thus Mary expressed with a tremulous tear.

Her words bore a magic that thrilled in his bosom;
   He found the fair damsel all thoughtful and lone:—
One vow—one embrace—and Lochleven's young blossom
   Has mounted his charger, and dashed in the throng!
O see you yon cavalcade far on the mountain
   By strath and by streamlet, fast, fleetful, and fair?
'Midst valour and beauty her danger surmounting—
   The Flower of fair Scotland in freedom is there!

TO THE RUINS OF CROOKSTON CASTLE,

RENFREWSHIRE.

Romantic Crookston ! thy time-stricken walls
  Do oft allure the pensive mind to stray
To the deep shades where solitude impals,
  In mournful gloom, thy mouldering fragments grey.
Meet theme art thou for his imperfect lay,
  Whose lyre is simple, while its tones are wild—
Who seeks not lofty language to portray
How Nature's charms his musings have beguiled,
In scenes where mountains rose, or verdant meadows smiled !

O rude memorial of the dreary past !
  Here, on thy upland throne, where winds are free,
Thou seem'st to frown upon the prospect vast,
  Like fallen pride, that frets its destiny :
And yet the summer sun smiles warm on thee ;
  The woodland loads the breeze with fragrance sweet ;
The winged warblers sport from tower to tree;
From distant glades is heard the lambkin's bleat,
And wild luxuriance all pervades thy lone retreat.

Here busy Fancy claims her own domain,
    And stays the hour when weary mortals sleep.
Lo! Superstition, with her magic train,
    Around thy walls their fearful vigils keep;
Fantastic forms parade the thorny steep,
And horrid sounds from unknown dungeons swell;
    In pale array does abject Beauty weep;
Anon wild shouts and clash of arms prevail—
Betimes the awful pause reveals the captive's tale.

Forsaken Crookston! in thy waning hours
    The curious eye, at this far distant time,
May trace, in thy rude lineaments and broken towers,
    What fair proportions graced thy golden prime.
    The bard has strung for thee a plaintive rhyme;
The rustic sings a fond regret for thee;
    The traveller leaves his weary path to climb
The devious way, to linger thoughtfully,
And scorn the savage hand that first dismantled thee!

The iron hand has revelled in the hall;
    The stately roof is prostrate in decay
That echoed oft, in times long gone, the call
    Of bugle-horn, when Lennox led the way
    Of horse and hound, and many a huntsman gay.

To rouse the fleet ones of the forest far ;
   Or, eager viewing in the distance grey,
The beacon's gleam, the harbinger of war,
Bade thee awhile adieu, and sped the vengeful car.

From tangled forest, or from tented plain,
   They turned to thee—a bold and gallant horde,
To win the pleasures of thy glad domain,
   Or wake the clamour of the festive board,
Where plaided chieftain sat and mail-clad lord,
   In chivalry's array, in jovial mood,
And Beauty smiled her victor knight restored,
Well were their pains who won for guerdon good.
The blue-eyed Scottish maids those merry chieftains woo'd !

And she sojourned here in gladness once,
   Whose fate persuades the frequent tear to start ;
Whose kingdom was a sad inheritance,
   Whose fatal gift—a too confiding heart !
   If things inanimate could truth impart,
Her injured fame might yet serener shine.
   The lettered voice of falsehood would depart,
And all confess how guiltless she did pine ;
So constant to her faith—would it had been divine !

And, near the blazing hearth, a modest reveller,
   With bowl in hand—the Baron's kind behest—
He sat at even-tide, the way-worn traveller ;
   An unknown stranger, yet a welcome guest.
   But all are gone !—they to their dreamless rest,
Fair Scotland's chivalry, and Beauty's pride
   And soon will Ruin stoop *thy* rugged crest ;
Yet gay Romance will o'er thy cairn preside,
And raise a fame for thee, to nobler piles denied !

THE STORY OF LIFE.

O FAIR are the waters that mirthfully glide
From their mystical home on the sunny hill-side,
Or valley, or meadow, or echoing grot,
From spoilers secure, and from cities remote.
Beautiful waters! so gentle and bright,
So joyfully leaping, they burst into light;
Fond tributes of Nature, abundantly given
To temper the burning refulgence of heaven.
Affectionate waters! through sunshine and song
They sprinkle the sward as they wander along,
And lave the long tresses, and cheer the young flowers,
Murmuring the joy of their primitive hours.

Onward—while kindred rejoicers draw near,
Enlarging its form, and to speed its career,
The streamlet in beauty and minstrelsy glides
Where Nature in fairest adornment presides;
Night stays not its journey the forests among,
Sweet cadence it gives to the nightingale's song,

Save when in the wildwood it lingers to sleep
In the secret recess where the willow trees weep—
O'er moorland, through greenwood, by night and by day,
Those waters go gaily and gladly away.

But ah! their rejoicing endures not for ever,
The songs of the streamlet are lost in the river.
When sullied and mournfully wanders the tide
Through the dark frowning haunts of ambition and pride;
And few are the gleams on their marge that remain
Of the scenes of past joy they can never regain,
Ere the waters of fountain, and streamlet, and river,
In the turbulent sea are entombed, and for ever.

For ever! O deem that betimes they return
From the darkness and toil of their comfortless bourne,
To the sunny hill-side, and the echoing grot,—
The valley, or meadow from cities remote,
When thither descending, in freshening showers,
They lave the long tresses and cheer the young flowers,
As they did in the joy of their primitive hours!

Like those waters' career is the story of life—
From gladness to gloom, from affection to strife.

The smiler that basks on its mother's fond breast
Is glad—a joy-giver, a blessing—and blest ;
But soon to the youthful endearers of home
The harbinger dreams of futurity come,
While the glee of the hall, and the game of the field.
In little misfortunes their warnings may yield—
Earth's fitful allurements but beckon them on
To desolate pathways, to journey alone,
Where high hopes will wither, and faithless depart
The visions of bliss, the fond dreams of the heart !

And when the lorn wanderer toils 'midst the strife
That ever prevails through the ocean of life—
When his long-cheated vision must cease to survey
The thoughts, scenes, and friends of a happier day,
And a mantle of sorrow around him is cast—
O 'tis good to recur to the beautiful past,
And cherish the tribute that memory pours—
The spirit to soothe in its loneliest hours !

SHE TOLD NOT HER SORROW.

Her heart was forlorn,
   Yet she told not her sorrow,
Nor the pangs that were borne
   On the wings of the morrow.
She loved! she believed
   That *his* vow was assurance;
But her faith was deceived,
   And it mocked her endurance.

She loved, (O that gleams
   Of such love should be slighted;)
But our happiest dreams
   Are the first to be blighted.
She marked a gay band,
   Then her spirit did falter,—
A wealthier hand
   He will press at the altar.

She heard in her grief
    The bridal bells pealing;
Still sought no relief
    In the charm of revealing.
She strove to refrain
    From her weeping and sighing,
Till her heart burst in twain:—
    O serene was her dying!

THE IMPROVIDENT.

Forlorn and wan, and full of grief,
   I leave a world of woe,
And seek my happy childhood's scenes,
   (Its days I ne'er can know ;)
But turn in anguish and despair,
   At Fate's severe decree—
All, all is desolation here—
   There is no home for me !

The genial bonds of kindred love
   I ever must forego ;
No lingerer from affection's band
   Is here to calm my woe.
The very walls frown on me now,
   That echoed once my glee ;
I cannot weep, though rends my heart—
   There is no home for me !

THE IMPROVIDENT.

The rustic hearth gleams not for me,
    And cheerless is the town ;
I have not strength for useful toil—
    I dread the rich man's frown.
My star of hope that brighten'd long
    The future's awful sea,
Has set for ever to my soul—
    There is no home for me !

Then bring me not philosophy,
    Its uses to define,
Nor eloquence, nor soft appeals,
    To teach me to resign—
A broken heart—and penury !
    What matter I am free,
Or what is life itself ? and yet
    Not any home for me !

Ha ! now I triumph o'er the past—
    Our hamlet's ivy'd fane !
(To Heaven the poor improvident
    Will ne'er complain in vain.)
The peaceful grave, that bourne serene,
    Bid all my sorrows flee ;—
Come, cheer my heart, we must be glad—
    There is a home for me !

TO A HOUSE FLY.

WRITTEN IN WINTER.

Poor, shivering, little wanderer,
   Whither on vent'rous wing ?
Where hast thou been this many a day ?—
   Thy story say or sing.

Hast thou in some warm crevice slept
   Since the ten thousand fled,
And here to wait till they come back,
   A heavy wager laid ?

Ah ! that were sure a foolish task,
   A wild design and bold,
For ill would suit thy little frame
   The dangers of a cold.

Perhaps thou art a traveller
   Our wintry homes t' explore ?
O then thou art a sturdy wight
   To brave our northern shore !—

Then take thy notes—and rightfully;
    Let's see what hast thou there—
" The window panes are cold, and such
    A piping in the air!

" The folks go shivering out and in,
    Or creep beside their fire,
And of their usual clamouring
    They never, never tire."

But no—thou art a homeless one,
    A sort of Wandering Jew—
Could I but spy thy little beard,
    I'd vow my guessing true.

Or art thou come, thou curious one,
    With thy inquiring stares,
To see how, in these biting times,
    A humble poet fares?

Go then with thy discovery,
    And say to them that sent,—
" He harpeth on right cheerfully,
    And diets with content."

But I'll suppose, frail one, thy lot
    To mine a semblance bears;
Thou art a friendless wanderer,
    And hast thy little fears:

Then welcome to my shelter—stay
    And share my little mess;
I love thee in my solitude,
    Ev'n for thy loneliness.

There! nestle in my sugar bowl,
    And sip what pleaseth thee:
Thank Heav'n that, of its kindness, sent
    Enough for thee and me!

A DREAM OF LOST JOY.

I had a bright glimpse of the time,
    When my spirit was joyous and free,
When I dwelt in the Highlander's clime,
    And sported in innocent glee.

I dreamed—I was tortur'd with joy—
    For I woke to a bitterer sense
Of a sorrow that knows no alloy,
    And a heart that's bereft of defence.

I stood on the scenes of my youth,
    The friends of my childhood were near,
All pictured in beautiful truth,
    The sportive, the sage, the severe.

So ardently lov'd and carressed,
    I felt like a being adored;
While round me they eagerly pressed
    To welcome their wand'rer restor'd.

For I had been lost to their care;
Afar I had strayed, and by night—
There was no one my danger to share,
And no one to guide me aright.

The night had been stormy and drear,
The wilderness dismal and wild;
The wolf-cry fell oft on my ear,
As onward I mournfully toil'd.

And long had they sought me, nor slept;
And where could their helpless one roam?
And often they prayed and they wept,
To have their young wanderer home!

And she, the sweet charmer, was there—
My beautiful love, and my first;
She wept in the common despair,
Till her young heart was ready to burst.

She tenderly drew me aloof,
And weeping, and smiling, she strove
To chide me, in gentlest reproof,
As a truant to duty and love:

Besought me, when next I would stray,
    To call her away for my guide,
She'd lead me the prettiest way,
    And homeward by evening-tide.

A tear marked her lingering care—
    I kissed it away—she approved;—
I braided her beautiful hair,
    And sung her the songs that she loved.

Then we pictured a happier day—
    A cot on some highland hill-side:
O I'd be a shepherd so gay,
    And she'd be my dutiful bride!

I woke by excess of my joy—
    I woke to a harrowing sense
Of a sorrow that knows no alloy—
    Of a heart all bereft of defence.

Those scenes are still fair to the view,
    But comfort for me they have none;
Those pleasures I ne'er can renew—
    The friends of my childhood are gone!

A DREAM OF LOST JOY.

And she, who was faithful as fair,
 Is wed to a happier mate ;
From pity alone can she spare
 A tear for my lonely estate !

Ye dreams of my scanty repose,
 Your images torture my head,
O cease, for my grief to disclose,
 The joys that for ever have fled !

THE MOURNER'S SONG.

O lay me down to rest in peace,
   Prepare my dreamless pillow ;
I long to be where sorrows cease :
   Beneath the friendly willow :—
Where through my heart no more will move
Or fear, or hope, or joy, or love !

Fear : if acquaintance reconciles
   Spirits of adverse form,—
Cheerful might I encounter toils,
   Nor dread each threatening storm ;
But Fear sits brooding o'er my heart
To aggravate the coming dart !

Hope : she subdued my anguish long,
   But I have lost the maid ;
Grown wearied of her soothing song
   She sought a milder shade ;

And cold Despair, in triumph wild,
Expunged the promise she beguiled!

Joy: once I knew—the season brief,
    But so intense the measure—
Had it been less, I'd less in grief
    Bewail the absent treasure.
Wise man reproves the simple boy,
But envies still his store of joy.

And Love: the gentle flame, decayed.
    Has left me dark and lone;
Betraying once, and now betrayed,
    'Tis meet I'm now undone:
But O how sad it is to prove
No one that loves—and none to love!

Then I would lay me down in peace
    Upon a dreamless pillow,
For all the pangs of sorrow cease
    Beneath the friendly willow—
There will my stricken heart remove
From fear, and hope, and joy, and love!

STANZAS.

How should I murmur at the hour
When Death will lend his soothing power ?
    How should my soul complain
To part this fragile tenement,
By every striving passion spent,
    And grief subdued in vain ?

Should I be loth to yield this breath,
Or dread to meet the pangs of death ?
    Alas! the pangs of life
Have more of pain, even were they brief;
Nor long endurance brings relief
    From pangs of mortal strife !

Wearied and worn—I do not sleep ;—
Oppressed with grief—I do not weep—
    The grief that melts in tears
Exhales and dies :—but tears nor sighs
The bosom yields when once the prize
    Of wild and mortal fears !

Oh, I will murmur not to see
The shaft that brings me liberty;
   Nor will my soul complain
To part its dreary home, and rest
Where passion will no more molest,
   And grief pursue in vain!

LINES

WRITTEN IN AN ALBUM.

Awake once more, thou simple lyre,
   Thine artless cords have long been mute,
And faded all thou hadst of fire,
   That gave a voice to lover's lute :
What time I swept thee oft and free
To themes of mountain minstrelsy.

Yet once again, and I presage
   For thee, a long—a lasting rest :
Thy latest tones are booned a page,
   At youthful beauty's high behest—
And must I strike in vain ? ah me !
Departed is thy minstrelsy.

My lyre ! when for thy minstrel boy
   Thy wild notes won a rustic wreath,—
Ere I could raise my song of joy,
   I cast thee on a Highland heath ;

Doom'd to forsake lov'd forms and thee,
For scenes unkind to minstrelsy.

Sweet Lady! thou hast deigned to ask
   Of me some tributary lay;
Though much unworthy of the task,
   I've mused an idle hour away.
A witless rhyme I give to thee,
Alas! it has no minstrelsy.

When thoughtfully thine eye will trace
   The pages of thy cherished lore,—
Say, will it linger *here* to bless
   The cheerless lyre that wakes no more?
O scorn not its simplicity,
It knows no better minstrelsy.

May thy pure joys long yield thee smiles,
   As merry and as free as now;
May'st thou ne'er feel misfortune's wiles,
   Nor anxious care impress thy brow—
O may thy days as gladsome be,
As might be wished in minstrelsy!

THE TEAR-DROP OF JOY

To weep is not always a token of sorrow,
    Nor sadness alone can a tear-drop beguile,
For a moment of bliss from the heart's fount may borrow
    A symbol more sacred to joy than a smile.

In grief we may weep for a dear one departed—
    In care, when the soothings of hope disappear;
And mourners, who languish forlorn, broken-hearted,
    Have only one balm in their sorrow—a tear!

But the tear-drop of joy has a better emotion,
    More tiny in form, and more bright in career;
It has less of revealing, and more of devotion;
    'Tis a visible thought of what most we revere!

With a smile it is oft sweet companionship keeping,—
    Twin-spirits they seem, every ill to destroy.
Dear ——, if e'er 'tis thy lot to be weeping,
    May the tear which thou shed'st be the tear-drop of joy.

FIRST LOVE.

SERENE is Nature's majesty,
 And beautiful her pride,
When Summer brings her loveliness
 To meadow, tree, and tide.
And as serenely beautiful,
 The young enthusiast deems
The form that prompts his waking thoughts,
 And charms his fondest dreams,
What time his heart glows warm beneath
 First love's enchanting beams.

The voice of birds—the gush of brooks—
 Young flowers—the milky way—
Moonlight upon the midnight deep
 When winds have died away!
The radiant smiles of infancy—
 Soft music's magic wile—
Remembrance of departed joys
 And Hope's illusive guile :—
These have a soothing influence
 Through life's enduring toil !

O these have pleasing influence
　　And gentle aid impart
To win from cold Despondency
　　The care-worn pilgrim's heart—
But, in the sweet spring time of life
　　More pleasant far may prove
Than aught of beauty or delight
　　Around us, or above,
The genial, the bewildering power
　　Of first and faithful love!

The mourner may forget his tears,
　　And sorrow yield to mirth;
The Exile may in time forget
　　The fair land of his birth:
Friendship decays—remembered scenes
　　Erewhile in memory set—
Joys that have cheered a lonely hour—
　　Griefs, well remembered yet—
May be forgot—but first fond love
　　What heart can e'er forget?

TO THE FALSE.

TRUE is thy memory, beauteous one!
   For, in our happy days,
Thou'st told me oft how good it was
   To search its dreamy maze:
When we compared, in converse sweet,
   Within our own fair grove,
The bygone joys of childhood,
   And the present ones of love!

True is thy memory, once beloved!
   But is it still as pure,
As it was wont to be, when thou
   My wanderings would'st allure
To worship in the woodland path
   The radiance that would float
In the beaming of thy peerless eye?
   Methinks that it is not!

True is thy memory, faithless one!
    Is it not to thee now
The record—ah, the lasting one—
    Of many a broken vow?
And can'st thou now, in solitude
    At the calm hour of even,
Think on the past without a pang,
    Beneath the eye of Heaven?

True is thy memory, hapless one!
    In a gay and mirthful crowd
I saw thee pass—thy cheek was pale—
    Thou only *would'st* be proud;
In that fair throng one heart did beat
    That once was all divine,
But now entombed in sorrow's gulf—
    O wherefore was it *thine?*

LUGANO.

If waters that serenely lie
Beneath an ever placid sky,
Where Summer loves to linger long,
And sunny hours their stay prolong :
If mountains, robed in loveliness,
That meet the sky with soft caress :
Fields, ever fertile, ever fair,
And fragrant groves, and healthful air :
If Nature's various charms combined
To form a beauty undefined
With blessing can a scene invest,
Lugano, thou'rt supremely blest !

For seldom fairer galaxy
Will greet the pilgrim's wondering eye ;
Or beauty and magnificence,
That win the eye and charm the sense
Invite with more persuasive tongue
The homage of the poet's song.

Thy lofty hills, majestic piled,
Were else tremendous, dark, and wild,
But for the bland fertility
That beautifies their majesty;
And varied hues of verdure blent
On terrace, vale, and battlement,
Beguiling with a warm embrace
And kind—like maiden loveliness
That fondles with an angry sire,
And turns to love his wildest ire.

Thy lake, methinks, a tranquil tide
Assumed by Nature in her pride,
To image, in its varied blue,
The fairest sky she ever drew!

The blooming mead, and mossy cell,
The vineyard rich, and golden dell,
Proclaim that all the seasons smile
To bless the happy Switzer's toil.
I envy not his heart who roams
Afar from these delightful homes,
Where peace presides in hut and hall,
With heavenly freedom crowning all!

Scotland! my own, my native land,
I love thy soil from strand to strand;
In humble hut, in field, and fold,
In lake and stream, and mountain old,
I love thee in thy various forms—
I love thee in thy very storms;
And thank the destiny divine
That honoured me—a child of thine!

But prejudice, with hateful sway,
Shall never rule my humble lay,
When gift or grace of other clime
Induce the tribute of my rhyme.

Then will I murmur not to own
That richer woods than thine imbrown
The hills and plains of Swedish land;
Or how the common parent hand,
That gave peculiar charms to thee,
Gave others more fertility;
How sterner aspects far than thine
Preside on Alp and Apennine;
How sweeter flowers than thine arise
In radiance of Italian skies;
And every charm, combined, reside
By fair Lugano's silver tide.

THE BROKEN SWORD,

A TRADITIONARY TALE OF CULLODEN.

It fell on that eventful day
  The Stuart's hapless cause
Was blighted on Culloden field,
  By stern unyielding laws.

The fight was o'er—the vanquished bands
  Fled far to wood and wild;—
O many a tear was shed that day
  By father and by child.

The shades of even robed in gloom
  The oaks of old Duncan,
As by their pathless mazes sped,
  A wanderer from the plain.

He was from fell Culloden moor,
    And of the royal band,
Who, then dispersed, pursued the foe
    O'er the affrighted land ;
Destroying them—ah ! darkest deed—
    With wild and murd'rous hand.

His sword, deep dyed with Scottish gore,
    Was broken then in twain ;
One half was girded by his side,
    The rest was with the slain.

Onward he went—the green fields lay
    Four weary miles behind ;
The sun went down, the raven croaked
    To the loud, lamenting wind ;
Some shelt'ring covert was his need,
    But no one could he find.

And cold that wintry night came on,
    And dismal the forest grew ;
But the soldier's heart, so bold and brave,
    No idle terror knew ;
Yet he often thought of the carnage red,
    And the hardy men he slew !

And now the rain drops beat the sod,
    And the wind rushed fitful by—
The youth looked up—a-well-a-day!
    A fearful storm was nigh;
And yet no glimpse of friendly shade
    Broke on his wistful eye.

And soon the drenching torrent fell;
    The tempest bent the trees—
" Hark! was not that a female's voice
    Came wafted by the breeze?"

Few paces on the traveller went,
    When, lo! in a darksome maze,
A lovely form lay on the ground.
    " Kind Heaven, I give thee praise,
That led me here," the soldier cried,
    " This weeping one to raise."

He placed her by a sheltering bush,
    And wrung her tresses fair,
Then, fondly kneeling by her side,
    Bestowed a gen'rous care;
And, sooth to tell, it was her meed,
    For she was wond'rous fair.

Soon passed away the wintry gale,
    The storm subdued its might,
And, piercing through the greenwood veil,
    The moon shone warm and bright,—
As if in pity for that pair,
    Lone wand'ring in the night.

Then of the wanderer's mournful cause
    The soldier fain would know—
" O wherefore thus forlorn abroad,
    And why this bitter woe ?"

The storm had fled—the rain had ceased—
    The loud wind died away ;
The sweeping clouds, by sudden fits,
    Disclosed the moon's pale ray.

Then as the maid's returning strength
    The soldier's care repaid,
She murmured forth her pensive tale
    Beneath an oaken shade.

Not far, within the forest's bounds,
　　From other homes remote,
Young Flora's dwelling stood serene—
　　A fair sequester'd cot.

Her fathers, there, for ages past,
　　Had dwelt in peace secure ;
With cheerful toil, and rosy health,
　　Their little joys were sure.

Till civil discord turned to grief
　　The cheerful peasant's mirth—
Dissever'd many a friendly tie,
　　And darken'd many a hearth.

And how their household joys decayed,
　　The maiden wept to tell :
How first on fatal Sheriff-muir
　　Her father's kinsmen fell.

She told how, seven long years before,
　　A youthful brother went,
For England bound, on mission dire,
　　By secret conclave sent.

But tidings soon arrived that he
    And many more were lost ;
The vessel, in a storm, went down
    Upon the English coast.

Then stricken by the sudden grief,
    Her aged mother lay,
Nor left her bed of sickness once
    Until her dying day !

But calm content would still attend
    The husband's rural toil,
And joy within their humble home
    Appear'd once more to smile.

" Till O," she said, " our clansmen came
    Adown the hills in glee,
Their pibroch wail it was that brought
    This bitter woe to me !

" My father plumed his bonnet then,
    And girded his claymore ;
And took the targe our ancestors
    In many a conflict bore :

' I go to fight for my Prince's right,'
   In joyful mood, said he—
' But I'll return when the red coats mourn
   Our certain victory !'

" He gave my mother a parting kiss,
   And he gave me another,
And he bounded away ; but a fearful gloom,
   As he went, came o'er my mother.

" She drew me to her tender breast,
   And tearfully she said,
' May kinder fate avert the doom
   My vision'd eyes have read—
I saw thy father's lifeless form
   Upon a cold heath bed !

' But pray with me, my daughter,—pray
   That Heaven may be thy guide,
If e'er thou shou'dst, an orphan, stray
   On life's uncertain tide.'
She bless'd me with her parting breath,
Then slowly closed her eyes in death !

" With no one near to share my grief,
   I watch'd her all the night,
Till passing winds bore mournfully
   The pealings of the fight.

" And when they ceased, I long'd to know
   What to my sire befell.
Soldier !—in pity for my woe,
   Spare not the worst to tell !"

She said, and by the moonlight clear
   Her weeping eyes they bent
On the soldier's broken sword—to hear,
   O grief ! the loud lament
That wrung her sorrowing heart, as she
Fell faintly by the old oak tree !

———

A cot within a pleasant glade—
   A dwelling meet for joy ;—
No sound is heard save wood-bird's note—
   And waters murm'ring by.

A lovely solitude, without,
    In charm that never dies:
A dreary aspect reigns within—
    Pale death, and tears, and sighs!

Two youthful ones are lonely by
    The bier of a dead mother:
There is the maiden, woe-begone,—
    And there,—her long-lost brother:

For such was he, the soldier youth,
    Who, in the storm, that night
Descry'd and rais'd the weeping one
    When wandering from the fight.

He was not lost, as had been said,
    In times of discontent,
For he esponsed the royal cause,
    Nor did the dire intent

Which he set out to execute;
    And now with those came he
Who, on Culloden, fought for George,
    And won the victory!

A TRADITIONARY TALE OF CULLODEN.

Dim shone the morrow's sick'ning beams
    Upon Culloden heath,
The hopes and fears of yesterday
    Had left but grief and death.

And many a true and valiant heart
    Then found a desert grave,
While unavailing tears bewail'd
    The faithful and the brave.

It was a fearful thing to gaze
    Upon the scene around;
The perished flowers of Highland might
    Bestrewed the crimson ground;
The dew that sought the heather-bell
    On their cold breasts was found!

With dismal calls, and wailings loud,
    Resounding o'er the wild,
The mother sought her husband there,
    The father sought his child.

Amidst the slain were weepers twain,
　A plaided form attending—
Young Flora and her brother o'er
　Their father's corse were bending.

He lay like a fallen eagle there,
　His high brow dyed with gore ;
His hands outstretched : one grasped his dirk,
　The other his claymore,
Seven prostrate Southrons by his side—
Proofs of his valour ere he died !

Then fondly kneeling by her sire,
　To pray for his spirit fled,
The maiden from his breast withdrew
　The fragment of a blade.

One glance towards her brother's side—
　One piercing shriek—the last
That burst from that sweet maiden's soul,
　And all her griefs were past—
The steel that crush'd her father's life,
Her brother wielded in the strife !

THE HIGHLAND GARB.

WRITTEN FOR THE FIRST ANNIVERSARY DINNER OF THE HIGHLAND GARB SOCIETY. *

In the days when Scotia's fame was young,
  " A long time ago,"
Her Highland sons, in Highland garb,
  " Were dress'd from top to toe ;"
And well the plaided heroes graced
  Hill, forest, glen, and lea,
Like eagles of their mountain land,
  As noble and as free.

---

* Several years ago, an ardent desire to perpetuate the national costume of their ancestors prompted a few Highlanders in Glasgow to institute a society for that object, and the support of a charitable fund. From the excellence of the design, and the perseverance of its founders, the "HIGHLAND GARB SOCIETY" speedily flourished, acquiring eminent patronage and a large increase of members.

The first grand anniversary meeting took place in the Ossianic Hall, in the winter of 1839. The banquet was attended by several hundred Highlanders, all attired in the national garb. Few circumstances could have been better calculated to gratify a Highland heart than the display which was there presented. So great was the enthusiasm which prevailed on the occasion, that several natives of Ireland, rejoicing in Highland descent, came from their distant homes to participate in the harmony, and warm their breasts in the Garb of Old Gaul.

Fill high the cup, and be the toast,—
The Highland Garb of yore!
The Highland hills, the Highland hearts,
The pibrochd—the claymore!
   The Highland hills, &c.

For ages long that race has gone
   To many an honour'd grave:
By Fame enrolled as chief among
   The faithful and the brave;
And they are still as bold and true
   In their beloved domain,
Or where by adverse fortune led,
   In lands beyond the main.
   Fill high the cup, &c.

The Highland hearts are living yet,
   As noble as before:
But where are now the Highland garb,
   The pibrochd, the claymore,
The philabeg, the *cotagarr*,
   And all the fair array,
That cheer'd the friend, and scar'd the foe—
   O tell me, where are they?
   Fill high the cup, &c.

But will we let the ancient garb
   Our fathers lov'd, be gone ?
Or will we brook to see it borne
   By stranger forms alone ?
O no ! we will remember it,
   We'll cherish it most dear ;
And if we must its use forego,
   We'll prize it, to revere !·
     Fill high the cup, &c.

O yield again, ye Highland hills,
   Our fathers' ancient strains :
And their beloved, long-lost, attire,
   Restore, ye Highland plains !
Thy spirit has not slumber'd yet,
   Land of the minstrel's story,—
Land of the generous and brave,—
   Of gallantry and glory !
     Fill high the cup, &c.

SONG.

THE BANKS O' CLYDE.

AIR:—"*O' a' the airts.*"

By Clyde's clear stream a flow'ret grows,
    A flow'ret rich an' rare;
Nae lordly ha' nor mountain bower
    Can boast a flower sae fair—
O sweet are Scotland's maids, I ween,
    By mountain, glen, an' tide—
But nane can vie wi' her I loe
    Upon the banks o' Clyde.

It is na for her saft red lips,
    Nor for her sparklin' een;
It is na for her gentle form,
    Nor yet her artless mein;
But O it's for her mind sae pure,
    Adorned in angel pride,
That I hae sighed an' pined wi' luve
    Upon the banks o' Clyde.

SONG.

O brightly fa' the mornin' rays
    Upon the leaves o' June,
An' sweetly warbles in the wud
    The linty's evenin' tune ;
But brighter far the kindly glance
    O' Mary at my side ;
An' sweeter far her voice to me,
    Upon the banks o' Clyde.

Let Fortune frown upon my lot,
    Or a' her gifts bestow,
She ne'er can change the constant flame
    That burns thro' weal an' woe.
Then wheresoe'er my steps be led,
    An' whatsoe'er betide,
This faithfu' heart will linger lang
    Upon the banks o' Clyde.

THE WANDERER.

AN ILLUSTRATION OF A POPULAR SYMPATHY.

Embower'd within a pathless wood,
A place of shade and solitude,
   Where crowded many an ancient oak,
And many a wild-flower bloomed unseen,
   And only birds, and riv'lets broke
The stillness of the holy scene—
A peasant dwelt;—a hardy man,
Whose cheerful task it was to scan
The precincts of a rich domain,
Protect the forest's antlered train,
And, bending o'er the rooted soil,
To ply the axe—romantic toil!

To him a weary youth once came,
Of wasted form and weakly frame:
His vestments sad, yet trim and clean,
The measured step, and solemn mein,
The fallen cheek, and languid eye,
The upward look, and frequent sigh,

Told, that the hapless child was he
Of genius, and of—misery!

The rustic well the youth surveyed,
    And, wondering, waited his behest,
Who, unaccustomed rev'rence paid,
    And thus his plaintive tale expressed :—

" Lone dweller in the forest glade,
    Where peace and blest contentment smile.
To thee my random steps have strayed
    O'er many a long and dreary mile.
    Nor do I grudge my ardent toil
To meet with all my heart desired,
    Since, prompted by the musing maid.
Prospective fame my bosom fired.
For, lo! while yet a cherished boy,
Mine artless lyre was all my joy;
But manhood led me forth to strife,
And then I sighed for such a life
As Nature's favoured children know,
Whose days and years so smoothly flow
In woods and wilds—in nameless bliss—
Good truth! in such a scene as this.

"But longer I could not abide
My destiny's resistless tide;
And now I leave the city's noise,
To share with thee thy sylvan joys.
I come, 'tis true, in meek attire,
But bring ' my book, my scrip, my lyre.'
O, yield a home in yonder cot,
And say that Heaven has blessed my lot."

The peasant viewed the stranger's face,
Each mournful lineament to trace;
Nor, longer viewing, strove the less
His wakened feelings to repress:
Quoth he—"Young man, your case, I trow,
Is one of wondrous grief enow;
But, haste, relieve my anxious doubt—
Does your fond mother know you're out?"

EPISTLE TO A FRIEND,

ADVISING AGAINST THE PURSUIT OF POESY.

AN IMITATION.

Hail to thee ! Monarch o' guid fellows !
Gif thou be mortal, as they tell us—
I'll rax my pipe, an' croon my bellows
    To sing thy worth :
Thou art the winsomest o' billies
    Frae out the North.

" Hail to thee " is a sklentit phrase,
That's maistly gi'en to folk o' place ;
Atweel it is but empty praise,
    Aye bodin' flattery—
Sae I will e'en tak simpler space
    An' hamelier smattery :—

Guid mornin' to your sonsie pow,
Your honest phiz, an' bonny brow—
To you and yours I mak' my bow
      In richt sincerity,
Wishing ye a' the joys that flow
      Frae hame felicity.

May He wha ruleth ilka fate,
As weel the puir man's as the great;
Wha tents the mailen an' the State
      Wi' care divine—
May He protect frae evera strait
      Thyself an' thine!

Lang may ye live—lang may ye pree
The fruits that spring frae Honour's tree,
Lang smile in honest jollity,
      An', peacefu', calm,
O lang, lang, may ye ken the gree
      O' friendship's balm!

May never dark misfortune stress ye;
May never fellow-man oppress ye;
May never cankerin' care distress ye,
      Nor hardship's ban',
But may His guid benignance bless ye
      Wi' bounteous han'!

Noo for a wordie in your ear,—
Nae saunt nor mither's son sall hear :—
O' warldly guids an' usefu' gear
          Tak' tent, I rede ye,
An' for your ain dear sake forbear
          The rhymin' tradie.

Whan bodies envy Homer's fame
They should remember Homer's wame,
An' mony mair we needna name,
          E'en Homer's matches :
Parnassus speelers, lank an' lame,
          Puir feckless wretches !

O Poesy ! thou pleasing art,
Why is fell misery thy part ?
Why is't that he wha seeks thy mart,
          Ilk ill to brave,
Gets for his pains a broken heart
          An' scanty grave ?

If there is in this warl sae wild,
A wretch, frae evera joy exiled,
Misfortune's play-thing—misery's child—
          That's ane, weel mark—
Wha strives to live an' haud a bield
          On rhymin' wark.

Turn to the page o' bygane time :
How fared the sons o' song sublime ?
In evera age—in evera clime—
   A cheerless lot ;
Tears, an' a grave, an' then to shine :
   Their wrongs forgot.

Otway ! the gleams thou didst impart
Dissolved the eye, an' thrilled the heart :
But Taste once feasted wi' thine art,
   Gave puir return :
By penury's maist poignant smart
   Thou died forlorn !

Chatterton ! thine is a deathless name,
Yet *here* thou never kent a hame ;
The man wha doth thy frailties blame,
   Ne'er felt thy wounds—
Thy spirit to the world cried " Shame !"—
   An' burst its bounds !

O Fergusson ! thy Scottish lyre
In vain disclosed its halcyon fire :
Thy brain, with striving passions tir'd,
   In madness whirled—
Thou left, to seek some kinder choir,
   A heartless world !

But here the muse, wild, weepin', pale,
(Her blighted flowers she'll aft bewail,)
Will close the unregarded tale—
    'Tis vain to preach
To genius, if it will prevail,
    An' vain to teach.

Yet, Britain, boast na' o' thy store
O' classic worth an' minstrel lore ;
If ilk puir lad could leave the stoure
    Wha raised that fame,
Weel might thou tremble at the core
    Wi' vera shame!

LINES,

WRITTEN IN A CHURCH-YARD IN A LONELY SCENE OF THE HIGHLANDS.

TRAVELLER, in this wild solitude,
    Pass not all heedless on;
Bring here thy presence and thy thoughts,
    Devoutly and alone:

'Tis well to seek those heights sublime
    With pensive and admiring eye—
Those valleys speak of Nature's love,
    Those hills her gorgeous majesty.
But one who trod those haunts before,
    Or joyous youth, or thoughtful seer—
His journey past—his dreamings o'er—
    Came forth, and rested here.

Beauty and love, and rosy mirth
    Are nestled in yon little cot,
And pleasant toil, and calm content—
    Dost envy the poor peasants' lot?
Thou'lt miss them there in after days,
    Then should'st thou their new dwelling trace,
And know the measure of their joys—
    Seek this forsaken place.

THE HOURS I THINK OF THEE.

What time the Sun in purple pall is dying
   Afar beyond the eagle's aspired way;
What time the breeze through Flora's bower is sighing
   A solemn dirge for the departed day;
When on the mountain top the Queen of Heaven
   Smiles her bright path to stay the gloom of night;
When to the tempest-toss'd blest Hope is given,
   By the fair pole-star in celestial height:—
These are the hours I think of thee, most dutiful!
   The cold contentions of the world I leave,
   And dedicate, in thought, the glowing eve
To thee, my star of hope, my Beautiful!
And when the moon forsakes the mountain streams,
My thoughts pursue thee in a land of dreams!

THE NORE,

A FRAGMENT.

A burning sun shot through a cloudless sky,
   Pouring refulgence on a tranquil tide ;
   On slumb'ring sails the lively pennon died,
And Beauty slept on Ocean's majesty.

   Around an aged mariner we stood,
     List'ning to tales of carnage on the flood—
Of battles, and the Nore. In truth, we rested
     Where counselled once, for freedom and for fame,
     England's sea-warriors, when high the flame
They reared of Liberty ;—in days they breasted
     The yielding billows of remoter seas,
     Braving alike the " battle and the breeze,"
To tell of England, the supreme defence,
And speak her vengeful ire in thundered eloquence !

All silent now, and speckless : no commotion
   Breaks o'er the stillness of the placid tide—
The fairest sea that margins the dark ocean—
   A pleasant path, to joyful hours allied.
   *   *   *   *   *   *

LINES,

ON A VIEW OF THE COVENANTERS' TOMB IN THE BOG OF LOCH IN-KETT, GALLOWAY.

WHAT time Loch In-kett's distant wave is dyed
  By evening shadows in funereal gloom,
Why turns the wanderer from yon cairn aside—
  The Martyr Covenanters' desert tomb?

Here, in the dusk, the homeward rustic speeds
  From pallid forms in hoary, dim display;
Still, for his faith, the Good Enthusiast bleeds,
  When Superstition points her stern array!

Unwearied Thought! why vainly thus survey
  The seeming creatures Fancy loves t' invest;
No shade unholy e'er presumes to stray
  Where the blest ashes of the Martyrs rest.

POLITICAL ERROR.

Ours is, indeed, a fair and fertile land,
   And good it is its beauties to survey ;
   But the heart sickens when it chance to stray
From Nature's blessings to the ingrate band
Whose wild behest would madly strike the hand
   Of a good destiny. Deep discontent,
   And rudely told, with prompted anger blent,
Marks to the world the much-deluded train :
   But broader resteth the inglorious brand
On the base few, who, for a golden gain,
   Their unwise counsels, their deceit will vent,
To spoil the gladness of the meek domain :
Bidding the poor man's happiness depart—
Guiding astray the simple peasant's heart.

TRANSLATIONS

FROM

THE GAELIC.

THE AGED BARD'S WISH.

The following Gaelic poem, of which a translation has been here attempted, is certainly a curious and valuable relic of antiquity. That it was composed subsequent to the times of Ossian is manifest from the author's having adopted the pastoral style of composition, which does not appear to have been a characteristic of the Ossianic era.

This production is held in great estimation by native Highlanders, and deservedly so; for there is an ardour of enthusiasm and a force of expression pervading it, to which no translation can do justice.

More than one metrical version of the "Aged Bard's Wish" has, some time ago, appeared, though certainly none is deserving of notice excepting that of the late Mrs Grant of Laggan. But, in the opinion of the present translator, that lady must have met with a very garbled and mutilated copy of the original, as several stanzas have been totally omitted. And, without disparaging or depreciating her acknowledged merit, she appears occasionally, in her poetic enthusiasm, to have lost sight of the actual sentiments of the bard. Whatever may be deemed the merits or defects of the translation now offered, the author of it has been fortunate enough to obtain what he considers an entire and genuine copy of the Gaelic poem. He has also availed himself of a suggestion made by Henry Mackenzie, the Addison of Scotland, to Mrs Grant, (which she did not adopt,) by inserting the Gaelic original; and such of his readers as may happen to be conversant with the peculiarities of that language will, he flatters himself, feel disposed to make some allowance for the difficulties he had to encounter; for, in his zeal to adhere as rigidly as possible to the archetype, he has frequently found himself inevitably compelled to make use of words and phrases, which, if merely a matter of option, he would have avoided.

THE AGED BARD'S WISH.

I.

O ! lay me near the brooks which move
    So gently near the spreading tree,
To shade my languid head, above ;
    And thou, O Sun ! be kind to me !

II.

In tranquil rest I'll think or dream,
    While zephyrs fan my bank of flowers :
My feet laved by the wand'ring stream
    That o'er the plain serenely pours.

III.

The primrose pale, of grateful hue,
    The daisy, and the *ealvie* fair,
Shall deck my hillock, green with dew ;
    Inclin'd at ease, I'll ponder there.

MIANN A BHAIRD AOSDA.

I.

O càraibh mi ri taobh nan allt,
   A shiubhlas mall le ceumaibh ciùin,
Fo sgàil a bharraich leag mo cheann,
   'S bi thus a ghrian ro chairdeil rium.

II.

Gu socair sin 's an fheur mo thaobh,
   Air bruaich nan dithean 's nan gaoth tlà,
'S mo chas ga sliobadh 's a' bhraon mhaoth,
   'S e lùbadh tharais caoin tro 'n bhlàr.

III.

Biodh sòbhrach bhàn is àillidh snuadh,
   M'an cuairt do'm thulaich 's uain' fo' dhriùchd,
'S an neòinean beag 's mo lamh air cluain,
   'S an ealabhuidh' aig mo chluais gu h-ùr.

IV.

Around the valley's lofty brow
  Be blooming, bending trees inwove;
And warblers sing from many a bough,
  While rocks repeat their songs of love.

V.

From out the ivy-cover'd rock
  Shall new-born waters gurgling glide;
And sweet-toned Echo oft invoke
  The music of the constant tide.

VI.

May voice of hills and rocks prolong
  The joyous herds' endearing sound,
Then shall awaken, far and long,
  Their thousand lowings all around.

VII.

May sporting fawns be in my sight,
  By flowing stream or mountain breast;
The wearied kid, in mute delight
  And innocence, beside me rest.

IV.

Mu'n cuairt do bhruachaibh àrd mo ghlinn',
  Biodh lùbadh gheug a's orra blà;
'S clann bheag nam preas a' tabhairt seinn,
  Do chreagaibh aosd' le òran gràidh.

V.

Briscadh tro chreag nan eidheann dlù,
  Am fuaran ùr le torramam trom,
'S freagraidh mac-talla gach ciùil,
  Do dh' fhuaim srutha dlù nan tonn.

VI.

Freagraidh gach cnoc, agus gach sliabh,
  Le binn-fhuaim geur nan aighean mear;
'N sin cluinnidh mise mìle geum,
  A' riuth m'an cuairt domh 'n iar 's an ear.

VII.

M'an cuairt biodh lù-chleas nan laogh,
  Ri taobh nan sruth, no air an léirg;
'S am minnean beag de'n chòmhraig sgìth,
  'N am achlais a' cadal gu'n chéilg.

VIII.

Slow wafted by the gentle wind,
    The voice of lambs shall greet my ear :
Then anxious ewes shall answer, kind,
    When their approaching brood they hear.

IX.

O ! let me hear the huntsman's voice,
    On boundless heath, when hounds pursue !
Then will my heart again rejoice,
    And youth light up my cheek anew !

X.

Fresh vigour wakes me while I hear
    The horn, the hound, the whizzing bow—
Hark ! hark ! they shout—" Fall'n is the deer !"—
    I seem to skip by mountain brow !

XI.

Ah ! yonder is the faithful hound,
    My constant friend at night and morn ;
And, lo ! the rocks that would resound,
    In other days, my joyous horn !

VIII.

Sruthadh air sgéith na h-òsaig mhin,
   Glaodhan maoth nan crò mu'm chluais,
'N sin freagraidh a mheamh-spréigh,
   'Nuair chluinn, an gincil, 's iad a ruith a nuas.

IX.

A ceum an t-sealgair ri mo chluais !
   Le sranna ghăth, a's chŏn feagh sléibh
'N sin dearsaidh an òig' air mo ghruaidh,
   'Nuair dh-eireas toirm air sealg an fhéidh.

X.

Dùisgidh smior am chnaimh, 'nuair chluinn,
   Mi tailmrich dhŏs, a's chŏn, a's shreang,
'Nuair ghlaodhar—" Thuit an damh !"
   Tha mo bhuinn a leum gu beò ri àrd nam beann.

XI.

'N sin chi mi, air leam, an gadhar,
   A leanadh mi an-moch a's moch ;
'S na sléibh bu mhiannach leam 'thaghall
   'S na creagan a freagairt do'n dŏs.

XII.

The well-known cave now meets my gaze,
    Where generous shelter soothed by night :
How cheering was the log's warm blaze,
    While from the cup we drank delight !

XIII.

Then smok'd the feast, from mountains stored,
    While Treig's [2] clear wave would music pour :
Though spirits shriek'd and tempests roared,
    We slept secure, and scorned their power.

XIV.

I see Ben-ard of stately brow,
    'Midst thousand hills the chief, and best ;
The dreams of stags are on his prow ;
    The clouds repose upon his crest.

XV.

I see Scur-cilt above my vale,
    Where first the cuckoo tunes her voice ;
Where trees in lasting bloom prevail,
    And flowers and light gazelles rejoice.

XII.

Chi mi 'n uamh a ghabh gu fial
   'S gu tric ar ceumaibh roi 'n òidhch';
Dhùisgeadh ar sunnt le blathas a crann,
   'S an sòlas chuach a bha mòr aoibhneas.

XIII.

Bha ceò air fleagh bhàrr an fheidh
   An deoch à Tréig 's an tonn ar ceòl,
Ge d' sheinneadh tàisg 's ge d' rànadh sléibh,
   Sinnte 's an uaimh bu shèamh ar neoil.

XIV.

Chi mi Beinn-àrd is àillidh fiamh,
   Ceann-feadhna air mhìle beann,
Bha aisling nan damh na ciabh,
   'S i leabaidh nan nial a ceann.

XV.

Chi mi Sgorr-eild' air bruach a ghlinn'
   An goir a chuach gu binn an tòs.
A's gorm mheall-àilt' na mìle giubhas
   Nan luban nan earba, 's nan lòn.

XVI.

Let tender ducklings skim with speed
    The placid lake of stately pines,
Where stretches far the woody mead,
    And mountain-ash in softness twines.

XVII.

The beauteous swan of snowy breast
    Glides graceful o'er the yielding wave;
When soaring o'er the mountain's crest
    How lightsomely the clouds she'll brave!

XVIII.

Her stormy wing she oft hath led
    To frigid regions, distant, wide,
Where vent'rous sail may ne'er be spread,
    Nor oaken prow the wave divide.

XIX.

O Swan! from land of waves returned:—
    On mountain heights thy stay prolong—
And sing of thy affections mourned:
    I love to hear th' aërial song!

XVI.

Biodh tuinn òg a snàmh le sunnt,
    Thar linne 's mine giubhas, gu luath,
Srath ghiubhais uain' aig a ceann,
    A' lubadh chaoran dearg air bruaich.

XVII.

Biodh eal' àluinn an uchd bhàin,
    A snàmh le sprēigh air bharr nan tonn,
'Nuair thogas i sgiath an àird,
    A measg nan nial cha'n fhàs i tròm.

XVIII.

'S tric i 'g astar thar a chuain,
    Gu asraidh fhuar nan ioma' ronn,
Far nach togar bréid ri crann,
    'S nach sgoilt sròn dharaich tonn !

XIX.

Bì thusa ri dòsan nan tom,
    Is cumha' do ghaol ann ad bheul,
Eala' thriall o thir nan tonn
    'S tu seinn dhomh ciùil an aird nan speur.

XX.

Awake the soothing strain on high !
    Pour out the tidings of thy sorrow ;—
And Echo from the tuneful sky
    The woeful tale will fondly borrow !

XXI.

Now spread thy wings across the main—
    May fav'ring winds their aid impart !
O ! pleasant was thy parting strain—
    The love-song of thy wounded heart !

XXII.

O Youth ! [3] from what far distant shore
    Thy voice of sorrow, tempest borne ?
His journey he'll retrace no more,
    Who left my hoary locks forlorn.

XXIII.

Do tearful eyes *thy* grief bespeak,
    O Virgin ! of the whitest hand ?
May joy eternal bless the cheek
    That rests in the forgetful land !

XX.

O ! eirich thus' le t'òran ciùin,
   'S cuir naigheachd bhòchd do bhroin an cèill ;
'S glacaidh mac-tall gach ciùil,
   An gùth tùrsa sin od' bheul.

XXI.

Tog do sgiath gu h-àrd thar chuan,
   Glac do luathas bho neart na gaoith,
'S cibhinn ann am chluais am fuaim,
   O'd chridhe leoint'—an t-òran gaoil.

XXII.

Co an tìr on gluais a' ghaoth,
   Tha giulan glaoidh do bhroin on chreig ?
'Oigeir a chaidh uainn a thriall,
   'S a dh-fhàg mo chiabh ghlas gu'n taic.

XXIII.

B'eil deòir do ruisg O ! thusa rìbhinn,
   Is mine mais' 's a's gile làmh ?
Sòlas gu'n chrìoch do'n ghruaidh mhaoith,
   A chaoidh nach gluais on leabaidh chaoil !

XXIV.

O Wind! since faded is my sight—
    Where grows the reed of mournful sound?
It lives with those who shun thy might,
    And sport in liquid depths profound!

XXV.

O! raise me with an arm of strength;
    Beside yon birch let me repose;
At burning noon my wearied length
    May rest beneath its weeping boughs.

XXVI.

Then shalt thou come, O gentle dream!
    The stars of night shall be thy track;
In joyful music wilt thou gleam,
    And bring my days of gladness back.

XXVII.

See, O my Soul! the virgin fair
    Beside the monarch of the grove;
Her white hand 'midst her golden hair—
    Her mild eye on her youthful love!

XXIV.

Innsibh, o thrég mo shuil, a ghaoth',
   C'' àit' am beil a chuile' a fàs,
Le glaodhan bròin 's na bric r'a taobh,
   Le sgiath gun deò a cumail blàir.

XXV.

Togaibh mi—caraibh le'r laimh threin,
   'S cuiribh mo cheann fo bharrach ùr,
'N uair dh' eireas a' ghrian gu h-àrd,
   Biodh a sgiath uain' os-ceann mo shùl.

XXVI.

An sin thig thu O! aisling chiùin,
   Tha 'g astar dlù measg reull na h-òidhch',
Biodh gniomh m' òidhche ann ad cheòl;
   Toirt aimsir mo mhùirn gu'm chuimhn'?

XXVII.

O! m' anam faic an ribhinn òg,
   Fo sgéith an daraich, righ nam flàth,
'S a lamh shneachd' measg a ciabhan òir,
   'S a meall-shuil chiùin air òg a gràidh.

XXVIII.

He sings! she listens silently—
    Her heart pants to his tuneful breath—
Love gently speeds from eye to eye:
    The stag stays listful on the heath.

XXIX.

The sound has ceased! her bosom glows,
    And heaves upon her lover's breast:
Her lips, fresh as the stainless rose,
    Close to her lover's lips are press'd.

XXX.

May bliss await the lovely pair
    Who woke my soul to lost delight!
Bliss to her soul, that beauteous fair—
    The virgin of the ringlets bright!

XXXI.

Forsake me not: O dream of joy!
    Bring back, once more, th' ecstatic spell:
Thou wilt not hear: I sadly lie—
    O hills beloved, farewell! farewell!

XXVIII.

E-san a' seinn ri taobh 's i balbh,
  Le creidh leum 's a snàmh' na cheòl,
An gaol bho shuil gu suil a falbh,
  Cuir stad air feidh nan sléibhtean mòr.

XXIX.

Nis thréig am fuaim, 's tha cliabh geal mìn,
  Ri uchd 's ri cridhe gaoil a' fàs,
'S a bilidh ùr mar ròs gun smàl,
  Ma bheul a gaoil gu dlù an sàs.

XXX.

Sòlas gun chrioch do'n chomunn chaomh.
  A dhùisg dhomh m' aobhneas àit nach pill,
A's beannachd do t'anams' a rùin
  A nighean chiùin nan cuach-chiabh grinn.

XXXI.

'N do thréig thu mi aisling nam buadh ?
  Pill fathast—aon cheum beag—pill !
Cha chluinn sibh mi Ochoin ! 's mi truagh !—
  A bheannaibh mo ghraidh—slàn leibh !

XXXII.

Farewell! ye youthful company!
   Farewell! O Virgin, all divine!
The joys of summer bloom for thee—
   But winter's lasting chill is mine!

XXXIII.

O! bear me to the foaming tide,
   Where torrents fall with thund'ring roar:
A harp and shell be at my side—
   And shield my sires in battle wore:

XXXIV.

Then, O ye whisp'ring winds! draw near—
   O'er the dark deep, O friendly come:
And, to the Isle of Heroes,[4] bear
   My shade to its eternal home!

XXXV.

There, those who went of old, abide;
   They hear not music's soothing tone;
There Ossian old, and Daol reside,
   When night shall come, the Bard is gone!

XXXII.

Slàn le comunn caomh na h-òige
   A's òigheannan bòidheach, slàn léibh.
Cha léir dhomh sibh, dhuibhse tha sàmhradh.
   Ach dhomsà geamhradh a chaoidh.

XXXIII.

O! cuir mo chluais ri fuaim Eas-mòr
   Le chrònan a' tearnadh o'n chreig—
Bi'dh crùit agus slige ri'm thaobh,
   'S an sgiath a dhìon mo shinnsir sa' chath.

XXXIV.

Thig le càirdeas thar a chuain,
   Osag mhìn a ghluais gu mall,
Tog mo cheò air sgiath do luathais,
   'S imich grad gu eilean fhlaitheis.

XXXV.

Far 'm beil na laoich a dh-fhalbh bho shean
   An cadal trom gun dol le ceòl
Fosglaibh-sa thalla Oisein a's Dhaóil,
   Thig an oidhche 's cha bhi 'm bràd air bhràth.

XXXVI.

But ah! ere yet my shade will stray
    On Ardven, where the Minstrels dwell;
My harp and shell will cheer the way:
    And then, dear shell and harp, farewell!

XXXVI.

Ach O ! m' an tig i seal m' an triall mo cheò,
  Gu teach nam bàrd air Ard-bheinn as nach pill,
Fair cruit 's mo shlige dh-iunnsaidh 'n ròid,
  An sin, mo chruit, 's mo shlige ghràidh, slàn léibh !

NOTES.

The Poem is to be understood as the sentiments expressed by the Bard on his deathbed. He had lived to an old age in a state of pastoral simplicity; and now, on the eve of his dissolution, recalls those pursuits, scenes, and circumstances which afforded him delight in his early days.

Note 2, Stanza XIII. p 86.

" *Treig's clear wave* " ——— ———

Loch Treig is in the Braes of Lochaber. This may afford some evidence as to the scene of the Poem. *Ben—ard* and *Scur-cill*, mentioned in the succeeding stanzas, are now unknown; but the former (which signifies *high mountain*) may be the primitive name of Ben-Nevis; and the great waterfall, alluded to in the thirty-third stanza, may have been *Eas-bha*, in the same district.

Note 3, Stanza XXII. p. 90.

" *O Youth! from what far distant shore,*
Thy voice of sorrow, tempest borne?"

Tradition says that allusion is here made to a son of the Bard, who had perished on a foreign coast while on a warlike expedition. His grief has been awakened by the appearance of " the virgin of the whitest hand," who had been the betrothed of the departed hero.

NOTE 4, STANZA XXIV. p. 96.

———— " *to the Isle of Heroes bear
My shade*" ————

The ancient Celts believed Heaven to be situated in a beautiful island in the Western Ocean, where the sun went to repose in the evening, among the shades of departed heroes. They imagined that all the amusements in which they took delight whilst inhabitants of earth, were pursued without alloy in " Flathinnis," the island of the brave or noble.

It would be impossible to convey an adequate description of the Celtic paradise; but the following translation, from the effort of an ancient bard to impart some notion of its imaginary excellence, may be found interesting.

The Isle of Heroes.

In former days there lived in Skerr a Druid of high renown. The blast of wind waited for his commands at the gate; he rode the tempest, and the troubled wave offered itself as a pillow for his repose. His eye followed the sun by day; his thoughts travelled from star to star in the season of night. He thirsted after things unseen—he sighed over the narrow circle which surrounded his days. He often sat in silence beneath the sound of his groves; and he blamed the careless billows that rolled between him and the green " Isle of the West."

One day as he sat pensive upon a rock, a storm arose on the sea; a cloud, under whose squally skirts the foaming waters complained, rushed suddenly into the bay. From its dark bosom issued forth a boat; its white sails bent to the wind; around were a hundred moving oars; but it was void of mariners; itself seeming to live and move.

An unusual terror seized the aged Druid. He heard a voice though he saw no human form. " Arise! behold the boat of the heroes—arise, and see the green isle of those who have passed away!" He felt a strange force on his limbs; he saw no person; but he moved to the boat. Stepping into it, he exclaimed—" My foot in the barge of beauty: strange it would be if my heart were sad!"

The wind immediately changed — in the bosom of the cloud he sailed away. Seven days gleamed faintly round him; seven nights added their gloom to his darkness. His ears were stunned with shrill voices. The dull murmur of winds passed him on either side. He slept not, yet his eyes were not heavy; he ate not, yet he was not hungry.

On the eighth day the waves swelled into mountains—the boat rolled violently from side to side—the darkness thickened around him, when a thousand voices at once cried aloud, " The Isle, the Isle !"

The billows opened wide before him; the calm land of the departed rushed in light on his eyes. It was not a light that dazzled, but a pure, discriminating, and placid light, which called forth every object to view in its most perfect form. The isle spread large before him, like a pleasing dream of the soul; where distance fades not on the sight—where nearness fatigues not the eye. It had its gently sloping hills of green; nor did they wholly want their clouds; but the clouds were bright and transparent, and each involved in its bosom the source of a stream;—a beauteous stream, which, wandering down the steep, was like the faint notes of the half-touched harp to the distant ear. The valleys were open and free to the ocean; trees loaded with leaves, which scarcely waved to the light breeze, were scattered on the green declivities and rising grounds. The rude winds walked not on the mountains; no storm took its course through the sky. All was calm and bright. The pure sun of autumn shone from his blue sky on the fields. He hastened not to the west for repose; nor was he seen to rise from the east. He sits in his mid-day height, and looks obliquely on the noble isle. In each valley is its slow-moving stream. The pure waters swell over its banks, yet abstain from the fields. The showers disturb them not; nor are they lessened by the heat of the sun. On the rising hill are the halls of the departed—the high-roofed dwellings of the bards of old.

The original of this legend of Celtic mythology is contained in a very old and curious MS. in the possession of Mr Mackenzie, the Compiler of the " Beauties of Gaelic Poetry," &c. and will form part of an interesting Collection of Celtic Tales and Legends now preparing for publication.

THE DEATH OF CARRIL.

This Poem describes the tragical death of Carril, the bravest and most accomplished of the sons of Fingal, King of Morven.

Gaul, the most experienced warrior in the bands of Fingal, and only survivor of the royal race of Clan Moirne, of whom he held command under the famous flag and special advice of Fingal, was always honoured and regarded above any man of either clan. He occupied the seat next to the king, and enjoyed the best and most delicious messes. This, in his declining years, created the ill-will and aversion of the ambitious sons of Fingal —Carril in particular. Taking advantage of some difference which arose betwixt them at a banquet, Carril disputed the birth of Gaul by dint of arms. The champions entered the lists, and engaged each other in wrestling, whereby they could not decide the cause upon that day, the victory fluctuating betwixt them. The day following, they met, clad in armour, and furnished with sword and lance, contrary to the persuasion of Fingal. After both had shown much courage and bravery, Gaul gave the decisive stroke—Carril fell, mortally wounded, and was lamented by his father for many days. Gaul fled, full of grief, and concealed himself in a cave, not choosing to rely upon the friendship of Fingal till his days of mourning elapsed. The poem opens at the engagement, and ends with the lamentation of Fingal and the bards over the remains of Carril.

"Bas Chaireill" is taken from a manuscript collection made from oral tradition sixty-five years ago, and now in the possession of the Highland Society of Scotland.

THE DEATH OF CARRIL.

I.

In Tara's hall, (the hall of tuneful lyres!)
    The feast was spread [1]—the cup dispelled our woes!
'Twas then dissension woke the heroes' ire,
    And Carril mild, and mighty Moma rose.

II.

They rose to wrestle, and they strove with might,
    Their trampling sounded like the ocean's roar;
Loudly their bosoms panted in the fight;—
    The anxious nobles gazed in anguish sore.

III.

With fearful vigour now they twined and turned;
    Th' uprended earth yields to their tread away;
Throughout the day the furious conflict burned,
    And night descended on the equal fray.

BAS CHAIREILL.

I.

An taigh Teamhra nan cruit ciùil,
   Air dhuinne a bhi steach mu'n òl,
Dhùisg an iomarbhaidh na laoich ;
   Caircall caomh, a's Mòmad mòr.

II.

Dh' eirich gu spàirneachd na suinn,
   Bu truime na'n tuinn cùlg an còs
Sróinich an cuim' chluinnte cian
   'S an Fhiann gu cianail fo sprochd.

III.

Clachan agus talamh trom,
   Treachailte le'm buinn san strì ;
A' cliarachd rè fad an là,
   Gun fhios co dhiù b' fhearr sa' ghniomh.

IV.

Insatiate still : soon as the morn arose
    The heroes met, for mortal strife arrayed :
The sprightly Carril, vanquisher of foes,
    And Gaul the stern, renowned for piercing blades.

V.

In deadly clasp the champions now unite,
    Or, round their arms they speed in wild career :
The brave Fingalians mourned the dreadful fight,
    The clanging din resounded far and near.

VI.

Now flash their rapid arms with living fire—
    Their snowy breasts bedewed with liquid toil ;
Their tough spears shivered in the contest dire,
    Their targes cloven to the crimson soil.

VII.

Carril the kind, the valiant hero, fell :
    Breathless he lay beneath his portly foe ;
Fierce, cruel was the stroke—alas, to tell !—
    That, in the combat, laid the fav'rite low !

IV.

Air madainn an darra màireach
 Chaidh na suinn an dàil a chéile
 Caircall colgarra nam buadh
 Agus Goll nan cruaidh lann geura.

V.

Dh' iathadh, dh' iomaradh, agus thàirneadh,
 Iad gu nàisinneach sa' chumasg
 Gu cùidreach, cudthroamach, gàbhaidh.
 Bu chian le càch gàir am buillean.

VI.

Bu mhinig teine d'an armaibh
 'S cobhar garbh de'n cneasan geala
 Chaidh na sleaghan rìghne bhearnadh,
 'S an sgiathan gu làr a ghearradh.

VII.

Thuit Caircall caoin, calma, ceanal,
 Gun anail fo'n chruinne chròdha
 'S beudach, baòlach, bòrb, a bhuille
 Leag an curaidh sa' chruaidh chòmhrag.

VIII.

"Carril! my child! my own—my lovely boy!
  Thy wounds afflict thy sire, and many a friend!"—
Said Fingal, mournful in his altered joy:
  As mourns the sun, when wintry clouds impend.

IX.

"Carril! my darling! dreary is the hour!—
  Thine eyes are closed—thy teeth of whiteness fast—
Thy beauty altered like the faded flower—
  Thy strength departed like the desert blast!

X.

"Not ever more to seek the battle field
  Shalt thou, my fair, be seen with manly tread;
No more, young warrior, shall thy sounding shield
  Be heard, approaching to thy father's aid!

XI.

"Hads't thou been vanquished by a stranger host,
  Or by the Monarch of the World's [2] proud peers—
Then I'd revenge thy death, O Carril, lost!—
  Upon the Britons of triumphant spears!

VIII.

Mo laogh, mo leanabh, mo ghràdsa !
   'S truagh a chraidh do bhàs an t-athair
Gun robh Fionn na aignoadh cianail
   Bu truim' e na ghrian fo phlàthadh.

IX.

O Chaireill ! a mhic, a ruinean !
   Dhruid do shùil a's ghlàis do dheud-gheal
Ghluais do neart mar òsaig bhuamsa
   Chaochail do shnuadh mar blàà gheugan !

X.

Cha'n fhaicear ni's mò thu tighinn
   Air an t-slighe chum na còmh-stri,
Cha mo chluinn mi fuam do sgéithe
   'Ghaoil nam beum a tigh'nn do'm chòmhnadh.

XI.

'S truadh nach b'ann le ainneart choimheach
   No rìgh an domhainn a bhuailt' thu ;
'S bheirinn-sa' t'eirig a Chaireill
   Bho Bhreatunnaich nan arm buadhach.

XII.

" Repose in bliss ! thou graceful in the throng ;
Thou swept thy hundreds in the fields of fame ;
Far hast thou travelled—farther still has gone
The high renown thy deeds of valour claim.

XIII.

" Fair didst thou shine—enlivening and gay—
Amidst a hundred chiefs in Tara's hall ;
Oppressed with sorrow, we bewail to-day
Our dark bereavement—thy untimely fall !

XIV.

" Would thou had'st died amidst a battling throng,
Youth of the sparkling eye and auburn hair !
The race of Comhal would avenge the wrong,
And give the foe destruction and despair !

XV.

" The sad Fingalians raise their dismal strain ;
Their pride, their treasure, they must now deplore ;
For him does Fingal pensively complain,
Who in the heroes' hall can smile no more !

XII.

Beannachd leat a Chaireill cheutaich
   'S iomadh ceud a dhiong thu'n còmhrag
B'fhad a' thriall thu b'fhaide chliù ort
   Anns gach iùl an d' fhuair thu eòlas.

XIII.

Bu mhùirneach, misneachail, meanmnach,
   Thu 'n taigh Teamhra measg nan ceudan ;
A laoich fhuileachdaich san tòrachd
   Sgeula bhròin an diugh mar dheug thu !

XIV.

'S truagh nach ann an cath-nam mìlidh,
   Thuit thu mhìn-laich nan dual àr-bhuidh !
'S bhiodh sliochd Chumhaill toirt dhiù tòrachd
   Feadh gach ròid da'n leòn 'san àraich.

XV.

'S tùrsach, deurach, ceòl na Féine
   Caoidh an treun-laoch b' éibhinn gàire
'S tiomhaidh, doilich, Fionn ga d' bhròn
   Nach faicear beò thu 'n teach nan àrmunn.

XVI.

" Raise, Maids of Sorra ! raise your strains of woe
    For him, your fav'rite, in his early grave !
Pale as the mist that dims the mountain's brow,
    Ye tearful mourn the comely and the brave !

XVII.

" Oft on the pebbly strand he loved to stray,
    Or track the stormy deep in bold career ;
Oft in the chace, with many a soothing lay,
    He cheered the huntsmen when they roused the deer.

XVIII.

" But lowly now his stately form is laid,
    Stript of his armour and his fair array ;
Serene he slumbers in his narrow bed,
    By yonder mead, where weeping mourners stray.

XIX.

" Farewell, thou brave, best, beautiful, beloved !
    Active and eloquent,—in battle true !
A stream of strength thou, in the carnage, proved :
    Prince of the matchless blades—a last adieu !"

XVI.

Oighean Shòra seinnear bròn leo
    A leth an ògain chaoimh, àilidh,
Mar cheò nam beann tha gar muthainn
    'S snitheach, cumhach, ar lag mhàran.

XVII.

Air chuan nan leug is cian a ghluaisethe
    Thar sumainnean ceannbhan càir-gheal
Ceòlmhor, ceilcircach, 'san léirg,
    Ri linn scilg a taghach làn-dhamh.

XVIII.

Tha'n laoch fairechail, toirteil, calma
    Gun iomairt, gun àrm, gun uidheam
'S cumhann còmhnard t-ionad chomhnaidh
    An cois an Loin gur mor an pruthar!

XIX.

A laoich mheanmhnaich, mhùirnich, bhuadhaich,
    Labhraich, laidir, luainnich, bheuchdaich,
Mar shruth neart-mhor a measg nàmhaid
    Soiridh leat a ghràidh nan geur-lann!

NOTES.

Note 1, Stanza I. p. 104.

"*In Tara's hall, (the hall of tuneful lyres!)*
The feast was spread"———

"TARA," or, as it is sometimes written, "Temora," is supposed by some etymologists to be derived from "*Tigh-mor-rath*," i. e. "The house of the great circle." Should this derivation be correct, it is to be inferred that the form of the edifice was circular and spacious. However this may be, it is manifest throughout the whole poems of Ossian that it was a seat of royalty, and the resort of the numerous chiefs for conviviality, and relaxation after the fatigues of the chase, as well as for preparation for contemplated warlike exploits. When thus congregated, music and wine abounded. That these assemblies were very numerous is evident from the allusion made to Tara in the "Lament for Ossian," of which the following is a literal translation:—

"The numbers that were in my time,
In Tara of the sweet-sounding strings,
Were fourteen hundred and fifty,
Of our dear friends without blame,
Without mentioning the young king of Fail,*
Nor the wounded, the aged, and the young women,
Nor the youngsters who waited on the swords."

It is natural to suppose that on occasion of so many doughty chiefs being met, the rival princes would evince mutual jealousy of each other's bravery, which they would be disposed to exhibit to the utmost; the more particu-

---

* An abbreviation of "Innisfail," the primitive name of Ireland.

larly as the fair sex were witnesses of their prowess. An encounter, however, of such a nature as forms the subject of this poem, betwixt two individuals of such high repute, and held in such esteem, could not fail to be disapproved of by the more grave and sedate of those assembled, which the tenor of the poem shows to have been the case.

"*Tuneful lyres.*" In the original, "tuneful *cruits.*" "Cruit" is the name of a stringed instrument used of old in Scotland and Ireland, which was the same with the Welsh *crwdd* or crwth. For a long time past it has been confined to North Wales, so that the people of that part of the principality have been accustomed to consider it as being exclusively their own.

NOTE 2, STANZA XI. p. 108.

"*The Monarch of the World*"————

The Roman Emperor Severus, who died A. D. 211, is frequently distinguished by this title in the compositions of the ancient Celtic bards.

The following stanza of the Gaelic has been omitted in the translation, as conveying in substance the same ideas as in preceding verses. It is, however, given here in the original for the perusal of the Gaelic reader. It occurs as the sixteenth.

'S dosgach aig a ghaisgeach euchdail
    Thuit gun teugbhail anns a chumasg
    Mar neul oidhche ghluais e bhuaine
    'S e sin an sgeul truagh is cumhainn.

FAINASOLLIS.

The following Poem of Ossian is remarkable for its variety of versions, generally agreeing throughout in the narrative of incidents, but differing materially as to the catastrophe. This circumstance was probably inevitable, and may plausibly be accounted for from the oral transmission of the story through such a long series of ages. The present translator's inducement in having made preference of the version here given was on account of its superior beauty, and that its authenticity has been clearly ascertained so far back as the beginning of the seventeenth century. That it must at that period have been considered as the most genuine is evident from its having been recognised by John Mackay, a bard of the time, better known to Highlanders by the cognomen of "Piobaire Dall."* In order to gratify the curious reader, several of the different versions of the catastrophe of this poem are subjoined to it.

The following is an account, as traditionally given, of the incidents which occurred previous to the opening of the poem:—

Myro, son of the king of Sora,† sailing once along the Irish coast, came to a bay remarkable for its beautiful seclusion. Surveying the smooth expanse, he beheld a group of nymphs desporting themselves, as they thought, unseen, and enjoying the cool of the summer eve among the

---

* See his Address to Sir Alexander Macdonald of Sleat, in the "Beauties of Gaelic Poetry," in which the original of the following poem appears, as well as the information embodied in the preliminary narrative.

† *Sorcha* in the original. It is uncertain what island was known by this denomination in the times of Ossian. It may be supposed, however, to be one of the Orkneys, from the affinity betwixt the names. *Sorcha* was probably derived from two words, now obsolete, —*orc*, a whale, and *a*, an island : the Isle of Whales. The island is frequently mentioned in the poems of Ossian, and seems to have been noted for the cruelty of its inhabitants.

waters. For a time he fancied them daughters of the sea, and continued to gaze with admiration and awe; but observing, as he drew nearer, that their forms were entirely human, he made all sail to ascertain who they were. On seeing his approach, they hastened, with fear and modesty, to conceal themselves in the crevice of an adjoining rock. Determined to make captive of the fairest, Myro landed, discovered the ladies in their concealment, and carried off the most handsome. Suffused with tears, she implored him for liberty—telling him her name was " Faine-Soluis," (i. e. Beam of Light,) and that her father was king of that part of Ireland. Unmoved by her entreaties, he conveyed her to his boat, and bore her off to his own country. To her, however, Sora was a place of torment, the thoughts of kindred and home embittering every hour of her existence there. She at length formed the resolution of attempting her escape, and having one day sallied forth to the beach, as had been her custom, and observing Myro's pleasure-boat afloat, and no one within view, unmoored it, and, committing herself to the mercy of the elements, nimbly leaped on board. A favourable breeze having sprung up, she was driven upon the coast of Scotland, at a spot where Fingal and his attendants were refreshing themselves after hunting. Her eyes beamed with joy as she recognised the hero. After mutual salutations, she informed the King of Morven of what had happened, and, imploring his protection, as Myro was in pursuit, assured him of her determination to die rather than return. The sequel of the story is related in the poem.

FAINASOLLIS.

I.

As Fingal with a chosen train,
  By Roya's murm'ring Fall delayed,
They spied upon the misty main
  A bark that bore a lonely maid.

II.

And sooth, she was a gallant bark,
  And lightsomely on ocean sped,
Nor lingered, till she won her mark—
  The creek by Roya's loud cascade.

III.

Forth came a form of love and light,
  Fair as the beams of summer skies;
Like ocean's foam her bosom white,
  But ah! bedewed with tears and sighs.

FAINE SOLUIS.

I.

Là do dh' Fhionn le beagan sluaigh,
  Aig Eas-ruadh nan éibhe mall,
Chunnacas a' seòladh o'n lear
  Curach ceò agus bean ann.

II.

'S b'e sin curach bu mhath gleus
  A' ruith na steud air aghaidh cuain,
Clos cha d'rinncadh leis no tàmh
  Gus an d' ràinig e 'n t-Eas-ruadh.

III.

'S dh'eirich as maise mnà,
  B' ionann dealradh dh'i 's do'n ghréin,
'S a h-uchd mar chobhar nan tonn,
  Le fliuch-osnaich throm a cléibh.

IV.

Admiring, as the maid drew nigh,
    The princes stood upon the plain;
For wond'rous lovely to the eye
    Was she who now had left the main.

V.

Then tearful spoke that lovely one:—
    " If thou art Fingal, aid me hence:
Thy count'nance is the wanderer's sun—
    Thy shield, the helpless one's defence!"

VI.

In soothing voice the monarch said,
    " O beauteous branch in sorrow's blight,
If hardy swords can give thee aid,
    Our dauntless hearts will prove aright!"

VII.

" O, I'm pursued on yonder sea!—
    He comes—a chief of savage fame!
The son of Sora's king is he—
    Myro the Fierce, by rightful name!"

IV.

Is sheas sinn uil' air an raon,
  Na flaithean caoin a's mi féin ;
A bhean a thainig thar lear,
  Bha sinn gu léir roimpe séimh.

V.

" 'S mo chomraich ort ma 's tu Fionn,"
  ('S e labhair ruim am maise mnà)
" 'S i d' gnùis do'n ànrach a ghrian
  'S i do sgiath ceann-uighe na bàigh."

VI.

'S a gheug na maise fo dhriùchd bròin,
  'S e labhair gu fòil mi fhéin,
Ma 's urra gorm-lannan do dhion
  Bidh ar crì nach tiom d'an réir.

VII.

" Tòrachd a ta orms' air muir,
  Laoch is mòr guin air mo lòrg,
Mac rìgh Sorcha sgiath nan arm,
  Triath d'an ainm am Maighre bòrb."

VIII.

" Thy cause, fair wand'rer, I'll defend,
    Whoe'er he be would thee allure;
And in despite of Myro's might,
    In Fingal's hall thou'lt rest secure.

IX.

" The Hall of Rocks is near at hand,
    Where they, the Sons of Song, abide;
There generous cheer, and friendship bland,
    Await the wanderer of the tide!"

X.

Then came in view, like fleetful steed,
    A chief whose stature none excelled:
Ploughing the deep with angry speed,
    The very course the maiden held.

XI.

Tall were his masts, and white his sails;
    Swiftly he came, that sullen lord:—
" Welcome! proud rider of the gale—
    To Fingal's feast, or Fingal's sword."

VIII.

'S glacam do chomraich a bhean,
 Ro' aon fhear a th'air do thì ;
'S a dh'aindeoin a Mhaighre bhuirb,
 Bi'dh tu am bruth Fhinn aig sìth.

IX.

Tha talla nan creag aig laimh,
 Aite tàimh clanna nan fonn,
Far am faigh an t-ànnrach bàigh,
 A thig thar bhàrca nan tonn.

X.

Sin chunnacas a tighinn' mar steud
 Loach a bha mheud thar gach fear,
A caitheamh na fairge gu dian
 An taobh ciand' a ghabh a bhean.

XI.

B' àrd a chroinn, bu gheal a shiùil,
 Bu mhirc 'n t-iuil na cobhar sruth ;
"Thig a mharcaich nan steud stuadhach
 Gu cuilm Fhinn nam buadh an diugh."

XII.

With scornful eye, and haughty mien,
    And ponderous weapon by his side—
Ringing his shield with vauntful din—
    He came—defying, and defied!

XIII.

Gaul, royal Morni's son, advanced,
    And hurled his dart with sudden aim;
In speedy flight the weapon glanced,
    And clove th' intruder's shield in twain.

XIV.

Oscar arose to follow Gaul,
    (Whose might in battle ne'er was foiled!)
Arose the noble heroes all,
    Spectators of the onset wild.

XV.

Then Oscar in his fury sent,
    With his left hand, a fiery dart—
O fatal shaft!—O aim unmeant!
    It pierced the hapless maiden's heart!

XII.

Bha chlaidheamhe trom toirteil nach gann
　　Gu teann air a shlios gu réidh ;
Sgiath dhrimneach dhubh air a leis,
　　'S e 'g iomairt chleas air a chlè.

XIII.

Thug Goll mac Morna 'n urchair gheur,
　　A's air an treun do thilg e sleagh ;
B' i 'n urchair bu truime beum,
　　D'a sgéith do rinn si dà bhlòidh.

XIV.

Dh' eirich Oscar 's dh-eirich Goll
　　Bheireadh losga lòm 's gach cath,
'S dh' eirich iad uile na slòigh
　　A' dh' amharc còmhrag nam flath.

XV.

Sin thilg Oscar le làn-fheirg
　　A chraosach dhearg le laimh chlì
Do mharbhadh leis bean an fhir
　　'S mòr an cion do rinneadh l'ì.

XVI.

By Roya's Fall she's laid at rest,
  The Beautiful—the Beam of Light!—
Upon each lovely finger placed
  A golden ring—her royal right.

XVI.

Thiodhlaiceadh leinn aig an Eas,
   Fàine-solais bu ghlan lìth,
'S chúir sinn air barraibh a meòir
   Fàin òir mar onair gin rìgh.

NOTES.

A VERSION of the story of Fainasollis is to be found in a collection of ancient poems in the possession of the Highland Society of Scotland, which belonged at one time, as ascertained by an inscription on the MS. itself, to the Reverend James Macgregor, Dean of Lismore, the metropolitan church of the see of Argyle. It appears, from dates affixed to it, to have been written at different periods from 1512 to 1529.

This manuscript distinguishes the genuine poetry of Ossian from the imitations made of it by later bards, and ascertains the degree of accuracy with which ancient poems have been transmitted by tradition for the last three hundred years, during the latter century of which the order of bards has been extinct, and ancient manners and customs have suffered a great and rapid change in the Highlands. Some of the poems in this and other collections agree with pieces taken from oral recitation in different parts of the Highlands and Isles. The test which such an agreement affords, at a distance of so many centuries, of the fidelity of tradition, cannot but be curious to such as have not had an opportunity of observing the strength which memory can attain when unassisted by writing, and prompted to exertion by the love of poetry and song.*

The catastrophe in the story of Fainasollis, in the version given by the Dean of Lismore, mentions the fall of Myro (there called Dayro Borb) by Gaul after a severe conflict; the placing of a gold ring on each of his fingers after his death, and his interment near the waterfall: while Fainasollis lives, and sojourns a year with Fingal in Morven. The following is a literal translation of the concluding part of the poem in the collection referred to:—

> Gaul of the glowing spirit rushed on
> To hew down the hero, who stood as a rock of ice.
> Whoever should then behold them,
> Furious would seem the strife of death!
> The hand of Morul's son laid low
> The King of Sorn's son—tale of grief!

---

* See the Committee of the Highland Society's Report on Ossian.

NOTES.

> Sad were our people for the coming of the maid,
> On whose account the hero fell in dread affray.
> After the mighty had fallen
> On ocean's strand, O deed of woe!
> The daughter of the King of the wave-surrounded land
> Remained for a year in the land of Fingal.
> We buried, by the side of the water-fall,
> The man of might and of prowess;
> And we placed on the point of each finger
> A ring of gold, in honour of the King.

Macpherson introduces another version of Fainasollis, by way of episode, in the third Book of Fingal. There the lady is killed by a shaft from the bow of her pursuer, and Fingal himself avenges her death by slaying the ferocious Borbar, as Macpherson calls Myro. The following is a literal translation of the concluding part of the Gaelic poem adopted by that translator:—

> He (Myro) rushed on in his fury;
> He hailed neither Fingal or his people;
> The unerring arrow flew from his hand,
> And the maiden fell.
> The strife of mighty feats
> Bore down the King of Sora's son. O tale of woe!
> On the green mount was dug his tomb of stone,
> And over against it is the stone of the maid.

Which Macpherson renders thus:—

"The maid stood trembling by my side. He drew the bow: she fell. 'Unerring is thy hand,' I said, 'but feeble was the foe!' We fought, nor weak was the strife of death: he sunk beneath my sword. We laid them in two tombs of stone; the unhappy children of youth!"

An opportunity occurs here for easily contrasting the simplicity and distinctness of narrative in the ancient poem with the general and turgid expression of Macpherson's translation.

A third version occurs in Miss Brooke's "Reliques of Irish Poetry." The catastrophe in that lady's poem nearly coincides with the Dean of Lismore's, and with another edition preserved in a manuscript collection made by Mr Duncan Kennedy, in the possession of the Highland Society. Both Miss Brooke's and Mr Kennedy's versions include the death of Myro, or Moire Borb, by the hand of Gaul, the placing the rings on each of his fingers after death, and the lady sojourning a year with Fingal; but in the former, and in some other editions of the poem in the Society's possession, the story relates that Gaul remained six months getting his wounds cured under the care of that generous and hospitable king. Fingal's celebrity as a physician is indeed a favourite topic in many of the ancient tales and poems: to his magical cup, in particular, are ascribed many wonderful medicinal virtues.

STANZA XV. p. 124.

"*Then Oscar in his fury sent,
With his left hand, a fiery dart.*"

The Fingalians had a law, that none was to aid either party in a single combat with the right hand. Oscar took advantage of an exception to this law by hurling a weapon with his left hand.

FRITHIL.

THE poem here translated, although a composition of very great antiquity, breathes, in the original, such tenderness and simplicity as must enhance its attraction to the comparatively small number of readers who will be able to appreciate its inherent merits.

The classical reader will easily perceive the resemblance the story bears to that of Bellerophon as related by Homer; and it will be gratifying to some to observe the different manner in which incidents of such conformity are treated by the Great Father of poetry and a Highland Bard.

The scene of the poem is Loch Fraoch, about eleven miles west from Dunkeld, in Perthshire. The incidents of the tale are traditionally these:—

Frithil, young, brave, and accomplished, after having been betrothed to the daughter of Mey, a lady of rank and power, had the misfortune to become an object of that lady's own love. She discovered her passion to the youth; but being unable to prevail over him, determined, in revenge, that he should die. On a small island in the lake, then called Loch Mey, there grew a mountain ash, which was supposed to possess extraordinary virtues in its fruit,—serving both as food and physic. But none dared approach it, owing to an enormous reptile which constantly lurked at its base. Mey, relying upon the gallantry and courage of Frithil, contrived to send him within reach of the monster by feigning sudden illness, and requiring at his hands a cluster of the healing fruit. The object of terror chancing to be asleep, the bold youth succeeded easily in his enterprise. Disappointed in her purpose from that circumstance, the lady required that he should return to the island, and bring thence a ponderous branch, believing that the rustling of the leaves would inevitably rouse the monster. Frithil undertook the task a second time, and was killed. The poem concludes with the lament of his love, who recites his virtues, bravery, and beauty. As if in fulfilment of her desire, expressed in the last stanza, the lake is now known by the name of the hero, and an ancient ruin on an adjacent eminence is said to have been the residence of Mey.

FRITHIL.

I.

The sigh of a friend on fair Frithil's repose :
    Alas ! the young hero is laid in his grave :
The sighs of our warriors their sorrows disclose,
    And our maidens lament him—the beautiful brave !

II.

Ah, see the fresh carn of our Frithil's decay,
    And why did the star of our gallants depart ?
He fell by the cruel deceiving of Mey,
    The mother ingrate of the loved of his heart.

III.

Weep on, ye fair maidens of Cruathan, weep on ;
    Severe was the fate that bereft ye of glee :
O weep, for your fav'rite for ever is gone,—
    The beautiful scion of heroes was he !

FRAOCH.

I.

Osna caraid air cluain Fhraoich;
    Och tha 'n laoch an caiscalcrò!
An osna sin on tùrsach fear,
    'S on trom galanach bean òg.

II.

Sud e siar an carn sa'm beil
    Fraoch mac Fhithich an fhuilt mhaoith,
Am fear rinn buidheachas do Mheidh:
    'S ann air a shloinnte Càrn-Fhraoich.

III.

Gul nam ban on chruachan shior,
    'S cruaidh an dàil a mhill an gean;
'S a dh' fhag an osna trom, trom,
    Fraoch mac-Fhithich nan colg sean.

IV.

But saddest is she who now weeps by his side,
  The daughter of Carol, the lovely and pure ;
Though many the heroes who sought her for bride,
  For Frithil alone her affections were sure.

Upon an island of Loch Mey,
  Fast by the southern shore,
There grew an ever-blooming ash—
  An healing fruit it bore.

VI.

Sweeter than honey to the taste,
  And pleasing to the gaze ;
Its reddened clusters would support
  A fasting one three days.

VII.

But danger lurked around, and woe
  To him who sought its power :—
A ven'mous monster at its root
  Had made its horrid bower.

IV.

Inghinn Chaireill 's grinne falt,
  Taobh ri taobh an nochd a's Fraoch ;
Ge h-ioma òigear thug dhi gràdh,
  Cha do ghràdhaich is' ach Fraoch.

Caoran do bhi 'n ì Loch-Màidh,
  Anns an tràigh tha sior fo dheas ;
Rè gach ràidhe agus mios
  Bhiodh a bharrach liont le meas.

VI.

Gun robh buaidh air a mheas dhearg
  Bu mhillse no mhil on bhladh ;
Gu'n cumadh na caoran bu dearg,
  Neach beò gun bhiadh car naoi tràth.

VII.

Ach bu chunnard 'dhol na dheigh,
  Ged bu luigh e chòbhradh na slòigh ;
Bha béist neimh 'a tamh ma bhun,
  'S bu bhaobhal a dhol da bhuain.

VIII.

A grievous sickness sudden seized
    Omath's fair daughter, Mey :—
"Now bring me Frithil here," she said ;
    He hastened to obey.

IX.

"Health ne'er will smile on me," she said,
    "Until I may command
An handful of the island fruit,
    Plucked only by your hand."

X.

"Such vent'rous effort ne'er was mine,"
    He said, and blushed the while ;—
"Yet for the mother of my love
    I'll cheerful risk the toil."

XI.

He went forth on his daring task
    And swam the waters free ;
Now, joy to tell, the monster sleeps
    Beneath the healing tree.

VIII.

Do bhuail easlainte throm, throm,
    Nighean Omhnaich nan còrn fiall ;
Chuireadh leatha fios air Fraoch.
    'S dh' fhiosraich an laoch ciod e miann.

IX.

Labhair i nach biodh i slàn,
    Mar faigheadh i làn a bos maoth
Do chaoran an Lochain fhuair,
    Gun aon neach d'a bhuain ach Fraoch.

X.

" Cnuasachd meas ni d' rinneam féin,"
    Thuirt mac-Fhithich nan gruaidh dearg ;
" Ged nach d' rinneam," arsa Fraoch,
    " Théid mi bhuain nan caor do Mhéidh."

XI.

Ach ghluais Fraoch air cheum gun àgh,
    'S chaidh e shnàmhadh air an Loch ;
Fhuair e bheist na siram-suain
    'Sa craos fosgailt suas ri dòs.

XII.

Unnoticed by the monster fell
    Young Frithil turned away,
And bore an armful of the fruit
    In joyful haste to Mey.

XIII.

" Thanks, generous champion, for your care
    My illness to destroy:
But this in vain—a heavy branch
    You bring, or else I die!"

XIV.

Once more he sped, the fearless youth,
    Once more he swam the lake;
But, ah! the death he 'scaped before
    Must now his path o'ertake!

XV.

He seized the mountain ash with might
    And tore a branch away,
But as he plunged into the lake
    The dragon barred his way;

XII.

Fraoch mac Fhithich nan arm geur,
    Thàinig e bho'n bhéisd gun fhios;
'S ultach leis do'n chaoran dhearg
    Do'n bhall an robh Meidh na tigh.

XIII.

"Ge math uil' na rinneadh leat,"
    Labhair Méidh bu ghille cneas,
"Chan fhoghainn leams' a laoich luain
    Gun a chraobh a bhuain á bun."

XIV.

Ghluais Fraoch gun gheilte cridh,
    A shnàmh air an linne bhuig;
'S bu deacair dha dh' aindeoin àigh,
    Teachd on bhàs anns an robh chuid.

XV.

Ghlac e na caoran air bharr,
    'S tharruinn e'n crann ás a fhreumh;
A' toirt a chasan da air tìr,
    Rug i air a rìs, a bhéist.

XVI.

O'ertook him as he spurned the wave,
    And grasped him in its gorge;
Young Frithil seized it by the jaw—
    Now for a sword to urge!

XVII.

The monster tore his arm away,
    And mangled his fair breast—
His love beheld—a dagger then,
    She bore in useless haste.

XVIII.

Wildly she sped, that lovely one,
    And plunged into the flood;
The woeful strife was ended then,
    The lake was dyed with blood.

XIX.

She reached the shore—there, pale in death,
    Her lover lay at rest;
Struck with her soul's deep agony,
    She fainted on his breast.

XVI.

Rug a bhéist air air an tràigh,
  Ghlac i a làmh steach na craos,
'N sin ghlac Fraoch is air ghiall :
  'S truagh ! a Thriath, gun sgian aig Fraoch.

XVII.

Chagainn a bhéist a chneas bàn,
  Leadair i a làmh gu leòn ;
Thàinig inghinn nan geala-ghlac,
  'S ghrad thug i dha sgian gu fhòir.

XVIII.

Cha robh a' chòmraig sin ach gearr,
  Bhuin e' n ceann d'i na laimh leis,
Fraoch mac-Fhithich a's a bhéist
  'S truadh a Thriath mar thug i ghreis.

XIX.

Gun do thuit iad bonn ri bonn,
  Air tràigh nan clach donn so bhos ;
'Nuair chunnaic an nighean a spàirn,
  Thuit i air an tràigh gun phlosg.

At last, awak'ning as from sleep, the maid
    Grasped in her palm the youth's dead hand of snow,—
Gazed wild around, like one imploring aid ;
    But none was near, and thus she told her woe :—

XXI.

"Burst, burst, my heart ! he's dead : my joy has ceased !
    (Alas ! he died not on the battle plain,
But fell, inglorious, struggling with a beast ;)—
    Now he is gone, I murmur to remain.

XXII.

"O he was lovely as the summer dawn ;
    His flowing hair was black as raven's wing ;
His cheeks were redder than the blood of fawn ;
    Softer than softest down was Frithil's skin.

XXIII.

" Whene'er he spoke his voice was sweeter far
    Than melody from minstrel's sweetest string,—
His eye more radiant than the brightest star,—
    His breath more fragrant than the breeze of spring.

'Nuair a dhùisg i as a pràmh,
  Ghlac i a lamh na laimh bhuig :—
" Ged tha thu' nochd 'n ad chomhdaidh eun,
  As mòr an t-euchd a rinn thu bhos.

XXI.

" 'S truadh nach ann an còmhraig laoch
  A thuit Fraoch le'm proinnte an t-òr !
'S tùrsach do thuiteam le béist,
  'S truagh nad dhéigh a mhair mi beò !

XXII.

" Bu duibhe na fitheach barr fhuilt,
  Bu deirge ghruaidh na fuil laoidh,
Bu mhèn' e na cobhar sruth,
  Bu ghille na'n cuithe corp Fhraoich.

XXIII.

" B' aird shleagh na crann siuil,
  Bu bhinne no teud chiùil a ghuth,
Snamhaiche bi fhearr na Fraoch
  Cha do leag a thaobh ri sruth.

XXIV.

" His shield was stronger than a gate of gold :
　　Heroes have sought the shelter of its frame,—
His sword was awful, as his heart was bold,
　　And Triumph smiled where'er the warrior came !

XXV.

" Good was the strength of his unconquered hand,
　　And good his swiftness in the rapid race :—
None could the valour of his arm withstand,—
　　None could outstrip him in the ardent chase.

XXVI.

" O he was lovely, and beloved by all :—
　　Lovely the cheeks that age was wont to bless ;—
Lovely the lips ne'er closed to friendship's call,
　　The lips that Beauty ne'er declined to press.

XXVII.

" We'll bear him, tearful, to his early tomb,
　　Where oft in solitude my tears shall flow ;—
To linger there, I leave a home of gloom ;
　　For he is gone, and nought remains but woe !

XXIV.

" Bu treis na còmhla sgiath,
   B' ioma triath a bhiodh r'a chùl.
Bu cho fad a làmh 'sa lann,
   'S bu mhath a dheann air a cùl.

XXV.

" Bu mhath spionnadh a dha làmh,
   'S bu ro mhath càil a dha chos,
Chaidhe aigne thar gach righ,
   Roimh churaidh riamh cha d'iarr fois.

XXVI.

" Ionmhuinn Tighearn, ionmhuinn tuath,
   Ionmhuinn gruaidh nan dearg ròs ;
Ionmhuinn beul nach diùltadh dàimh,
   D'am biodh na mnài a' tabhairt phòg.

XXVII.

" Togam a nis' gu cluain Fhraoich,
   Corp an laoich an caisealcrò
On bhàs ud a fhuair am fear,
   'S truadh mi mairean na dheigh beò !"

XXVIII.

"Henceforth these groves shall sound the mournful tale;
The Lake of Mey shall bear my lover's name;
And when with him I slumber in the vale,
His wrongs and mine shall every wood proclaim!"

XXVIII.

Air an doire thug iad ainm
 'S Loch-Maidhe air an Loch,
Far am biodh a bheist gach uair,
 'S a craos suas ris an dŏs.

EXTRACT FROM DERMID.

IN KENNEDY'S MANUSCRIPT COLLECTION.

I.

Thine eye was bluer than the berry
On the declivity of the mountain;
And milder the play of thine eyelids
Than the gentle breeze through the upland grass.

II.

Like the beams of the sun was thy hair,
Waving in auburn ringlets;
Thy skin was white as the foam:
O Youth! would thou hadst died on the battle-field!

III.

Mournful am I without the sound of joy,
But the notes of sorrow ever sounding;
The musical cruit of sweetest strain
Will never again wake my heart to joy.

AS-TARRUINN O' DHIARMAD.

BHO LEABHAR SGRIOBHAIDH LE D. C.

I.

Bu ghuirme do shuil na'n dearc
Air uilein nan leacan àrda
'S bu chiùine iomairt do rosg,
Na séimh osag air feur fàire.

II.

Mar dhrisinne gréine t' fhalt,
Am-lubach, cas-lubach, àr-bhuidh ;
Tha do chneas cho geal 'san cobhar,
A laoich ! nach d' fhoghainn na blàir dhut !

III.

'S dubhach mi gun iolach shòlais,
Ach turse bhròin a' sior cubhach
A chruit chiùil is binne mire,
Cha dùisg mo chridhe gu h-éibhneas !

IV.

My spirit has sunk into the gulph of waters,
Joyless and without repose, amidst their murmuring;
Constantly I meditate upon thy manners,
O! my arrow-wound of grief without cure!

V.

Never more shall I listen to thy converse,
Sweeter to me than the music of bards,
Or the thrush in the valleys of solitude:
For ever sad hast thou left my heart.

VI.

Never more shall thy countenance be seen
Shining in the Tower of Connal.
Alas! I am under a flood of dread—
When, my love! shall light beam on thee?

VII.

Dark is thy dwelling under the sod;
Narrow and frozen is thy lonely bed;
No morning will shine till the last,
That shall awake my love from his slumber!

IV.

Thuit m' aigneadh 'san aigeal stuadhach
Gun chlos no suaimhneas a' gàrraich ;
A sior chuimhneacha' do nòsan,
Och ! mo threoghaid bhròin gun àbhachd !

V.

Cha chluinn mi tuille do chomhra'
Bu bhinne na ceòl nam filidh,
No 'n smeòrach 'sna gleannain fàsaich
'S dubh a dh' fhag gu bràth mo chridhe.

VI.

Nis mo ch'an fhaicear do ghnuis,
A dhealradh gu h-ùr an tùr Chonail ;
Ochoin ! ni fo thuilteach ghabhaidh,
C'uin a thig a ghràidh ort solus ?

VII.

'S dorcha do bhruthan fo 'n fhòd,
'S cumhann, reòt, do leabaidh lom ;
Cha dhealraich madainn gu la bhrath
A dhuisgeas mo ghràdh an Sonn !

EXTRACTS

FROM

GAUL.

The lovers of Celtic literature are indebted to Dr Smith of Campbeltown for the preservation of this composition of Ossian, which, not only for high and impassioned poetry, but for delicacy and refinement of sentiment and feeling, is inferior to none of those translated by Macpherson. The original will be found entire in Dr Smith's "Sean Dana," and a translation into English by that compiler, in his "Gaelic Antiquities." In making mention of these works, (published in 1780 and 1787,) their unmerited neglect may be noticed as a cause of surprise as much as regret, especially when we consider the reception which Macpherson's translation met with, —a translator who, unlike Dr Smith, has on many occasions forfeited the praise due to literary integrity.*

In selecting a few passages for insertion in the present collection, the translator has followed the choice made by Henry Mackenzie, and embodied by him in the Report which he drew up concerning the authenticity of the poems of Ossian. Being fragmentary, it has been deemed superfluous to adhibit the corresponding Gaelic, and, from the peculiar style of the original, which, if it cannot be accounted blank verse, is very irregular and imperfect in numbers, it has been found impossible to render it in English rhyme without considerable deviation. The passages are therefore given

---

* Dr Smith, in corresponding with Henry Mackenzie, as Chairman of the Committee of the Highland Society appointed to inquire into the authenticity of Ossian's poems, said that he had been so much disgusted with the reception of his book as to have long banished the remembrance from his mind; and that he had not even kept a copy for his own use, to which he might refer for an answer to his queries. *Report*, p. 60.

literally, and line for line with the Gaelic. Some discrepancies from Dr Smith's translation will be discovered in words and lines; but it is humbly submitted that they will be allowed a preference on strict comparison with the original.

The preceding remarks apply also to the succeeding fragment from the "Lament for Ossian," which, as it is inserted less for the sake of its poetry than for the information it conveys regarding the manners of the Fingalians, has less claim to an effort at versification.

It has been deemed expedient to insert here a synopsis of the entire poem, to give the reader an idea of the continuity of the narrative :—

Fingal summoned his heroes for an expedition to the Isle of Ifrona. A flood in the river Strumon prevented Gaul from joining them in time; but he embarked in his ship, alone, on the succeeding day. On his voyage, however, he passed his friends, who were returning with victory, unperceived, and landed singly on the hostile shore. According to the chivalrous idea of those times, he would not fly, but struck his shield as a token of defiance to the islanders, against whom he singly maintained a desperate conflict, till, fearful of a near approach, they rolled a stone from above, which, striking his thigh, disabled him from moving; and there he was left by his enemies, dastardly alike and cruel, to pine and die. His wife Evirchoma, anxious for his fate, embarked in a skiff, with her infant son Ogall at her breast, in quest of her lord, whom she found in the pitiable situation described, and was able to carry to her boat, where they were discovered next morning by Ossian, who had sailed in quest of them, speechless and dying. He was only able to save the child.

EXTRACTS FROM GAUL.

OPENING OF THE POEM.

How mournful is the silence of Night
When she pours her dark clouds over the valleys!
Sleep has overcome the youth of the chace:
He slumbers on the heath, and his dog at his knee.
The children of the mountain he pursues
In his dream, while sleep forsakes him.

Slumber, ye children of fatigue;
Star after star is now ascending the height.
Slumber! thou swift dog and nimble,—
Ossian will arouse thee not from thy repose.
Lonely I keep watch,—
And dear to me is the gloom of night
When I travel from glen to glen,
With no hope to behold a morning or brightness.

Spare thy light, O Sun!
Waste not thy lamps so fast.
Generous is thy soul, as the King of Morven's:

But thy renown shall yet fade ;—
Spare thy lamps of a thousand flames
In thy blue hall, when thou retirest
Under thy dark-blue gates to sleep,
Beneath the dark embraces of the storm.
Spare them, ere thou art forsaken for ever,
As I am, without one whom I may love !
Spare them,—for there is not a hero now
To behold the blue flame of the beautiful lamps !

Ah, Cona of the precious lights,
Thy lamps burn dimly now : *
Thou art like a blasted oak :
Thy dwellings and thy people are gone :
East or west, on the face of thy mountain,
There shall no more be found of them but the trace !
In Selma, Tara, or Temora
There is not a song, a shell, or a harp ;
They have all become green mounds ;
Their stones have fallen into their own meadows ;
The stranger from the deep or the desert
Will never behold them rise above the clouds.

And, O Selma ! home of my delight,
Is this heap thy ruin,
Where grows the thistle, the heather, and the wild grass ?

---

* Alluding to the degenerate condition of the Fingalians.

Sorrowful under the drops of night,
Around my hoary locks,
Flutters the solitary owl ;
And the roe leaps from her couch,
Fearless of sorrowful Ossian.

Roe of the hollow carn
Where Oscar and Fingal have dwelt,
I will not do thee harm ;
Never shall my weapon wound thee.

To the height of Selma I stretch my hand :
But my home has no roof but the sky !
I seek my broad shield below,—
The point of my spear has struck its boss :—

Sounding boss of the battles!
I yet rejoice in thy sound ;
It awakes the days that are past,
And, in spite of age, my soul bounds·—

But away with the thoughts of war :
My spear is turned into a staff ;
It shall strike the bossy shield no more :—
But what sound is this which awakened it ?
A fragment of an age-worn shield ;
Its form is like the waning moon.

It is the shield of Gaul,—
The shield of the companion of my excellent Oscar.
But what is this that sinks my soul into gloom ?
Often, Oscar, hast thou received thy fame ;
But the hero of thy love shall now be the theme of song ;
O Malvina, with thy harp, be near !

DESCRIPTION OF EVIRCHOMA WITNESSING THE DEPARTURE OF HER HUSBAND.

In a light ship on raging billows,
The hero followed us on the second morrow.

But who is yonder on the rock, like mist,
Looking on Gaul through her tears ?
Her dark hair is waving in the wind ;
Her tender hand, like foam, among her locks.

Young is the son on her bosom ;
Sweet is her hum in his ear ;
But the blast has wafted away the song.
On Gaul, Evirchoma, thy love is fixed !

GAUL'S TENDER RECOLLECTION OF HIS WIFE AND CHILD, WHICH CROSSES FOR A MOMENT THE STERN UNYIELDING RESOLUTION NOT TO TURN HIS BACK ON HIS FOES, WHICH, WITH THE SUPERSTITION OF THOSE HEROIC TIMES HE SUPPOSES WOULD GIVE ANGUISH AND SHAME TO THE SPIRIT OF HIS BRAVE FATHER, MORNI.

Morni ! look down on me from the height.
Thy own soul was like the rapid stream
Beneath the white-crested foam of the boisterous strait.
So is the soul of thy son !
—Evirchoma !—Ogall !—
But the dear glimpse is not pleasant to the storm ;
The soul of Gaul is in the roar of battle !

Alas ! that Ossian, the son of Fingal, is not with me,
As he was in the time of Macnutha ;—
But my own soul is as a spirit of dread
That travels alone on the swelling seas,—
Pours a thousand waves on the trembling Isle,
And rides again in the chariot of the winds !

THE ANXIETY OF EVIRCHOMA.

What has detained thee, my love !
More than the others, in Ifrona ?
I am solitary on the shelving rock,
And Echo answers to my voice.

Mightst thou not now have returned
Though stress of sea had come over thee,
Thy thoughts being on the child of thy love,
Who pours with me the heavy sigh?
Alas! that thou dost not hear, my love,
The broken lisp of thy name
From the mouth of Ogall to speed thee home!
But I fear thou wilt never return!

EVIRCHOMA'S PERPLEXITY BETWEEN HER DESIRE TO GO TO THE ASSISTANCE OF HER HUSBAND, AND HER FEAR OF LEAVING HER INFANT BEHIND HER IN THE BOAT.

She glanced by the scanty beam
On the beautiful face of her son,
When about to leave him in the narrow skiff.
"Babe of my love! be here unseen!"

As a dove on the Rock of Ulacha,
Gathering berries for her little brood,
Often returns without tasting them
When rises the hawk in her thoughts;—
So three times returned Evirchoma.
Her soul as a wave that is tossed
From breaker to breaker, when the tempest blows,
Till she heard a voice of grief from the tree on the beach.

THE DEATH OF EVIRCHOMA.

His helmet was raised ; his locks were seen,
Disordered and in sweat.
My own grief awoke,
And he raised with difficulty his eye.
Death came like a cloud on the sun ;—
No more canst thou behold thy Oscar !

The loveliness of Evirchoma is darkened,
Her son holds the end of a spear, unconscious of grief.
Feeble was her voice, and few her words :
I raised her with my hand ;—
But she laid my palm on the head of her son,
Her sighs rising incessantly.

Dear child, vain is thy fondling—
Thy mother no more shall arise :
I shall myself be a father to thee ;
But Evirallin * is no more,
And who can supply the place of Evirchoma !

I feel the meltings of my soul return—
But why remember the sorrows that are past ?
Yet mournfully pleasant is their memory !

---

* The wife of Ossian.

CONCLUSION OF THE POEM.   FINGAL'S LAMENTATION OVER GAUL.

What is the strength of the warrior,
Though he scatter, as withered leaves, the battle?
To-day, though he be valiant in the field,
To-morrow, the beetle will prevail over him!

*   *   *   *

Prepare, O children of musical strings,
The Bed of Gaul, and his sun-beam * near him,
Where his resting-place may be seen from afar,
With lofty branches shading it;
Beneath the shelter of the oak of bluest foliage,
Of quickest growth, and most lasting hue,
That poureth its leaves on the breath of the shower,
While the fields around it are blasted.

Its leaves from the boundaries of the land
Shall the birds of summer behold,
And every bird, as it arrives, shall perch
On the top of its verdant boughs;
Gaul, in his mist, shall hear their warbling,
While virgins are singing of Evirchoma.

---

* The common term for a standard.

Until each of these shall perish
Thy memory shall not be disunited :—
Until the rock moulder into dust,
And this tree decay with age ;
Until the brooks cease to run,
And the source of the mountain waters be dried up ;
Until there be lost in the flood of age
Every bard, and song, and subject of story,
The stranger shall not ask, " Who is the son of Morni ?"
Or, " Where is the dwelling of the King of Strumon ?"

EXTRACT FROM BAS OISEIN,

(THE DEATH OF OSSIAN.)

IN KENNEDY'S MANUSCRIPT COLLECTION.

THE MANNERS OF THE HEROES OF FINGAL.

It is mournful to be to-night in the vale of Cona,
Without the voice of hound, and without music!
My heart is no longer cheerful,—
I am truly the old man and the feeble.

When we travelled to the vale of Cona,
Pleasant were our melodies by the way;
Many were the men of worth among us;
We were ever unwilling to offend.

When we ascended the heights of Cona
There were many, far and near,
To subdue the hart and the hind,
Many hundreds of which were never to rise.

Many were the heroes, when called upon,
To ascend the mountain with speed ;
Each with a naked spear in his grasp ;
A great sword and a shield.

Then did my beloved Fingal with his fifty chiefs
Meet in the lofty court :
His sun-beam, displayed on its staff,
Waved over them—a banner of victory !

Thence they would disperse afar
By the steeps of the mountain—
The powerful, courageous bands of Fingal :
Their bows ready in their grasp.

When the deer arose
We let slip our hounds in hundreds ;
Many a hart, roe, and hind
Fell, as far as I could view.

With our mountain spoils we returned at eve
To Tara of musical strings,
Where cruit and harp prevailed,
With many a bard to sing the tale.

Many a shell circled then,
Many were the new songs sung together,
Whilst the feast was consuming in the tower.
Beautiful and young were the Fingalian heroes.

Joyful were they in their accustomed course,
Musical, elegant, comely, valiant,
With wine, and flesh, their meed,—
Who were well beloved, and averse to falsehood.

The heroes, lovely, strong, and friendly,
Of great compassion and extensive fame,
Were generous and hospitable, and ever eager
To shield the stranger afar from his home.

In the day of battle, on the field of strife,
Mightier men never were heard of;
They would engage a man and a hundred;
Each Fingalian hero was a chief.

We never moved with reluctance
To give the impetuous battle,
That the forlorn might have the protection of valour,
And the wounded stranger the shelter of our shield.

The numbers that were in my time,
In Tara of the sweet-sounding strings,
Were fourteen hundred and fifty :
Dear friends of little blame,

Without reckoning the young King of Innisfail—
The wounded—the young virgins—
And the youths who attended the weapons.
Alas ! weak am I under grief,

Travelling the world to and fro,
And cannot discover one like Fingal.
In generosity and good fortune
None was ever found to surpass him.

The heroes have gone to the sunless grave ;
'Tis that has left mine eye as mist ;
I am like a wounded bird of the forest ;
I am comfortless, and weep in the hall :

Without sight, without offspring, or joy,
Like the tree that has ceased to grow,
Or the nut in its withered husk,
That is about to fall to the ground.

Grievous it is to the sorrowful heart
That it cannot derive comfort from a friend.
Like the dying hart is my form,—
My voice sinks under the dew of night!

OSSIAN'S ADDRESS TO THE SUN.

FROM THE ORIGINAL.

I.

O! thou who travellest on high—
    Round as the shield of chiefs of might!
Whence is thy brightness ever gay?
    And whence, O Sun! thy lasting light?

II.

In powerful beauty mounting high,
    The stars, retiring, own thee brave;
The moon, enfeebled, leaves the sky,
    To hide her in the western wave.

III.

Thou in thy journey art alone;
    Thee to approach there's none so bold;
From mountain height the oak has gone,
    And rocks give way when they are old;

DUAN DO'N GHREIN.

LE OISEIN.

I.

O Thusa fein a shiubh'las shuas !
 Cruinn mar lann-sciath chruaidh na'n triath,
Cia as a tha do dhearsa gun ghruaim,
 Do sholus a tha buan a ghrian ?

II.

Thig thu ann ad' àille threin,
 A's falaichidh rèultan uainn an triall,
Theid gealach gun tuar o'n spèur,
 'G a cleith fein fudh stuaidh 's an iar.

III.

Tha thusa ann ad astar amhàin,
 Co tha dàna bhi 'n ad chòir ?
Tuitidh darag o'n chruaich àird,
 Tuitidh carn fudh aois, a's scòrr ;

IV.

The ocean ebbs and flows again ;
 The moon is lost in upper skies ;—
But thou thy victory dost maintain—
 Glad in thy light that never dies !

V.

When dark'ning storms the world surround,
 When thunders roll, and lightnings fly,
Thou look'st in beauty from the sound,
 And smilest in the troubled sky !

VI.

But ah ! for me thy light has ceased :
 Thy count'nance I behold no more—
What time thy yellow locks invest
 With gold the clouds o'er eastern shores,
Or when thou tremblest in the west
 In Ocean, at thy dusky doors !

VII.

But it may be, my fate is thine ;
 The mighty, once, enfeebled grows ;
From airy heights our years decline,
 And travel quickly to their close :—

IV.

Traighidh, agus lionaidh an cuan,
   Caillear shuas an Ré san spèur,—
Thusa d'aon a chaoidh fudh bhuaidh
   An aoibhneas buan do sholuis fein !

V.

'Nuair a dhubhas mu'n domhan stoirm,
   Le torran borb, a's dealan beithr'
Seallaidh tu a' d' aill o'n toirm,
   Fiamhghair ort am bruaidlean nan speur.

VI.

Dhom-sa tha do sholus faoiu,
   'S nach faic mi a chaoidh do ghnuis ;
Sgaoilcadh cùil, a's orbhuidh' ciabh,
   Air aghaidh nan nial san oir ;
Na'n uair a chritheas ann san iar,
   Aig do dhorsaibh ciar air lear.

VII.

Ach d'fhaodadh gu'm bheil thu mar mi fein,
   'S an àm gu treun, 's gun fheùm an àm,
Ar bliadhnaibh a' tearnadh o'n spèur,
   Ag siubhal le cheile gu'n ceann.

VIII.

Rejoice, then, in thy youth, O Sun !
   Rejoice, O King ! whilst in thy might :
Old age will dark and cheerless run,
   Like to the moon's vain, feeble light,

IX.

When through a cloud she scans the waste ;
   Or like the mist on mountain face ;
Or on the plain the northern blast ;
   Or the slow traveller in distress.

VIII.

Biodh aoibhneas ort fein, a ghrian !
  A's tu neartmhor, a thriath, ad òige.
'S dorcha mi-thaitneach an aois,
  Mar sholus faoin an Rè gun chàil,

IX.

'S i sealltuin o neoil air an raon ;
  San liath cheo air thaobh nan carn ;
An osag o thuath air an rèith ;
  Fear siubhail fudh brèid, 's e mall.

ULLIN'S ADDRESS TO THE SUN.

FROM THE ORIGINAL.

Hast left thy deep-blue pathway in the height,
    Thou Sun, unblemished, of the golden hair ?
Soon wilt thou pass the dusky doors of night,
    To seek the West—thy resting halls are there !

The timid waves come slowly round to view
    The bright-faced one, and raise their heads with fear.
They see thy beauty when thou slumber'st, too,
    And weakly speed—afraid to linger near !

Take thou, O Sun ! thy rest without annoy ;
And may thy steps, returning, be in joy !

DUAN EILE DO'N GHREIN.

LE ULAIN.

An d'fhag thu gorm astar nan spèur,
  A mhic gun bhèud, a's òr-bhuidh ciabh ?
Tha dorsa na h-oiche dhuit reidh,
  Agus pailliun do thaimh san iar.

Thig na stuaidh mu'n cuairt gu mall,
  A choimhead an fhir, a's glaine gruaidh,
Ag togail fo eagal an ceann,
  Re d'fhaicinn co aill' a'd' shuain.
Teichidh iadsa gun tuar o d' thaobh.

Gabhsa codal na d'chòs tha dorch,
  A ghrian ! as pill an tòs le eibhneas.

MALVINA'S DREAM.

FROM THE ORIGINAL.

I.

It was the dear voice of my love!
    He came to me on smiling beams;
O wherefore does his presence move
    So seldom to Malvina's dreams?

II.

But I am tired of lingering here,
    Fathers of Toscar! hear my call:
Malvina's hast'ning steps are near—
    Open for me your airy hall!

III.

I heard his dear voice in my dream!
    I feel the fluttering of my soul;
Soon shall his presence more than seem;
    Soon shall I leave this cold control!

IV.

Why didst thou come, O cruel breeze,
    From gloomy waves, to cause my smart?
Thy wild wing rustled in the trees,
    And bade Malvina's dream depart!

V.

But she, the while, beheld her love;
    His robe of mist did winds unfold;
His skirts with sun-beams were inwove:
    They glittered like the stranger's gold.

VI.

It was the voice I loved so well!
    Though few to me thy visits be,
Yet in my spirit dost thou dwell,
    O son of Ossian, lost to me!

VII.

Does morning gild the azure height?—
    Its earliest beams my sighs attend;
Does evening moist the paths of night?—
    O, with its dews my tears descend!

VIII.

Oscar! I seemed, ere joy was past,
    When in thy sight, a pleasant tree,
Till death came like a desert blast,
    And bore thy life and love from me!

IX.

Spring brought again its gentle showers,
    But not a leaf of mine arose;
And summer spread again its flowers,
    But still Malvina felt her woes!

X.

The maidens marked my soul's annoy;
    They saw me silent in the hall;
They, friendly, touched the harp of joy,
    But still Malvina's tears would fall!

XI.

" And why," they said, " art thou forlorn;—
    Thou first of Lutha's maids so bright!
O, he was lovely as the morn;
    And he was stately in thy sight!"

AISLIN MHALMHINE.

'S e guth anaim mo ruin a tha 'nn
O ! 's ainmach gu aislin Mhalmhin' thu !

Fosgluibh-se talla nan speur,
Aithra Oscair nan cruaidh-bheum ;
Fosgluibh-se doirsa nan nial
Tha ceumma Mhalmhine gu dian !

Chualam guth a' m' aislin fein,
Tha fathrum mo chleibh go ard !

C'uime thanic an ossag a' m' dheigh
O dhubh-shiubhal na linne od thall ?
Bha do sgiath fhuimnach ann gallan an aonaich,
Shiubhall aislin Mhalmhine go dian.

Ach chunic is' a ruin ag aomadh,
'S a cheo-earradh ag aomadh m' a chliabh :
Bha dearsa na greine air thaobh ris
Co boisgal ri or nan daimh.

'Se guth anaim mo ruin a tha 'nn !
O ! 's ainmach gu m' aislin fein thu !
'S comhnuidh dhuit anam Mhalmhine—
Mhic Ossain is treine lamh !

Dh'eirich m' osna marri dearsa o near ;
Thaom mo dheoir measg shioladh na h'oiche !

Bu ghallan aluin a't fhianuis mi, Oscair !
Le m' uile gheuga uaine ma m' thiomchiol :
Ach thanic do bhas-sa mar osaig
O'n fhasach, us dhaom mi sios.
Thanic earrach le sioladh nan speur,
Cha d'eirich duill' uaine dhamh fein !

Chunic oigha me samhach 's an talla
Agus bhuail iad clarsach nan fonn ;
Bha deoir ag taomadh le gruaidhan Mhalmhine ;
Chunic oigh me 's mo thuiradh gu trom :—

" C' uime am bheil thu co tuirsach, a' m' fhianuis
Chaomh Ainnir-og Luath-ath nan sruth ?
An ro e sgiamhach mar dhearsa na greine ?
Am bu cho tlachdor a' shiubhlal 's a chruth ?"

THE END.

www.ingramcontent.com/pod-product-compliance
Lightning Source LLC
Chambersburg PA
CBHW032145160426
43197CB00008B/783